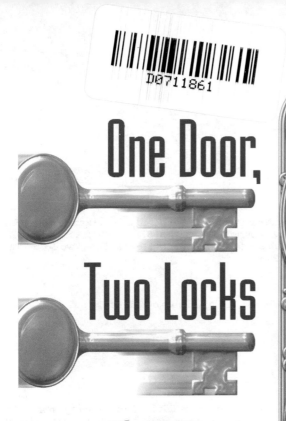

One Door, Two Locks

The 7 Keys to Unlocking the Door to Success in All Areas of Your Life

Dr. Jim Muncy

M ETAPHOR PRESS

This book is a derivative work with substantial overlap based on an original book, *A Few Keys to All Success*, by Jim Muncy, copyright 2002: ISBN 0-9722197-0-6. *A few Keys to All Success* remains in print. The author retains the copyright to *One Door, Two Locks*. The publisher of record is Metaphor Press.

One Door, Two Locks
The 7 Keys to Unlocking the Door to Success in All Areas of Your Life

By Dr. Jim Muncy

Copyright © 2009 by Jim Muncy
Published by Metaphor Press

All rights reserved, including the right to reproduce this book or portions herein in any form whatsoever, to include print, photocopying, audio, video, or electronically via ebooks or the Internet, without written permission from the publisher.

Printed in the United States of America
First edition as *One Door, Two Locks* January 2009

ISBN 13: 978-0-9822549-0-5

Published by Metaphor Press
10427 Orange Grove Drive
Tampa, FL 33618

Distributed exclusively through High Mountain Marketing
140 S. Main Street
Brooksville, FL 34601

Quantity discounts available
Cover design and layout by Parry Design Studio

CONTENTS

CONTENTS

FOREWORD

We all need encouragement. Sometimes we need soft and gentle words of encouragement that will comfort us as we heal our hurting soul. Other times we need strong words of encouragement that will push us to face the challenges of life head on. The trick is getting the right encouragement at the right time.

Author and motivational speaker Steven Covey tells a story that illustrates this point. One Sunday morning, Covey was on a subway train in New York. A man and his children boarded the train. The man sat down next to Covey and the children ran wild. These kids were irritating everyone in the car. The man just sat there in his own world, letting his kids run totally out of control.

Eventually, Covey could take it no more. He turned to the man and gave him *strong words of encouragement*. In a firm voice, Covey asked the man if he would please do something to control his children.

The man looked at Covey and realized he was right. The kids were misbehaving. Then he told Covey that they were coming from the hospital where, just an hour earlier, his wife—the children's mother—had died. When Covey heard this, he immediately realized this wasn't the time for strong words of encouragement. He apologized and began giving *soft words of comfort*.

At that moment, Covey's subway companion didn't need strong encouragement. He needed soft comfort. There are times, however, when just the opposite is true. Soft and comforting words keep us from getting up and moving on in life.

Back when I was playing sports, I was glad the team had trainers and not just coaches. The job of the coach was to push us through the pain. The job of the trainer was to help us heal. Coaches never cared how bad we hurt. They recognized that injuries were just part of the game.

But if you're writhing on the floor with a compound fracture of the leg, you don't want the coach to come out to you. He'll tell you to stick the bone back in your leg and get back in the game. You need a trainer who will let you protect the leg as it heals. Once you're healed, he'll hand you back over to the coach, who will again push hard and challenge you to move beyond the pain.

Yes, soft words of comfort are important for us to heal. However, soft words will never help us get up and be all we can be. The strongest trees are the ones that face the fiercest winds. The storms make them strong.

We all need strong words that will encourage us to face the storms of life.

In the pages of this book are *strong words of encouragement*. I am convinced that these are words that all of us need to hear. Strong words push us forward to get all we can from life. It's not that I am oblivious to the need for softer words at times. It's just that this isn't one of those times.

There is a time to lie down, rest, and heal. There is also a time get up, move forward, and see how much we can get out of life. If now is your time to move forward, then let's explore together the seven keys that will unlock the doors to all success in your life.

INTRODUCTION

*When one door closes, another opens; but we often look
so long and so regretfully upon the closed door that
we do not see the one which has opened for us.*
—Alexander Graham Bell

ONE DOOR, TWO LOCKS

I recently received an email from a former student named Ashley. Here's what it said:

"Something was always with me when I left your classes. I found myself starting to grow as a person and looking outside the little world I was trapped in. At the time, I was engaged to be married, but I was very unhappy in this relationship. I was being abused both physically and emotionally. I felt like I had such little to live for and nowhere to go. Your class said so much to me. I realized that I had dreams and goals that I had set for myself, and there was no way I was going to achieve these aspirations while being in so much pain. Soon after I graduated, I quit my job and broke off the engagement. I took off to find not only a job but a place where I was going to be successful, challenged, and genuinely happy. I did just that. I am doing something that makes me very happy and I have reached the goals that I have set for myself when I first moved here. I have gone through two promotions. I am now setting new goals along the way."

Prior to this email, Ashley was going nowhere. She was living in pain, and all that was ahead of her was more pain. Then, in just a few short months, her thinking began to change. When it did, the whole direction of her life began to change.

WHAT SUCCESSFUL PEOPLE KNOW

Here's the interesting part of this story. The class that Ashley took that changed her thinking was Professional Selling. How could a class on sales so dramatically change someone's life? Because this was no ordinary class in sales. Here's why I say that.

Several years ago, I decided to climb down out of my ivory tower and talk to people who were actually doing what I was teaching. I was teaching selling and so I talked to every salesperson I could find. I would take them to lunch, sit next to them at church socials, meet them after work, and so forth. I wanted to know what they thought it took to succeed in the world of selling.

These salespeople told me about prospecting, presenting, listening, closing, handling objections, building relationships, servicing after the sale, and the like. These were the exact topics I discussed in my sales classes. For a short while, that gave me a nice warm fuzzy feeling inside. I patted myself on the back because I was teaching my students exactly what every salesperson seems to know.

This warm feeling quickly cooled when I realized something. Remember, I said that I talked to every salesperson I could find. I didn't just talk to successful salespeople. Sure, I talked to some who were doing quite well and enjoying what they were doing. However, I also talked to some who were miserable and struggling just to get by.

That's when the painful truth hit me. The struggling salespeople knew just as much about what I was teaching as did the really successful ones. Obviously, there was something else to success in sales. There had to be something that successful salespeople knew that unsuccessful people didn't. I wanted to know what that something was.

As I dug deeper and made comparisons between the successful salespeople and those who were struggling, here is what I discovered: Successful salespeople understand sales strategies and techniques... but *so do unsuccessful salespeople*. Simply understanding sales won't make you a success in sales. Successful salespeople also understand key principles to all success. Unsuccessful salespeople do not. The difference was NOT a lack of knowledge of *sales strategies*. The difference was a lack of knowledge of *success strategies*.

ONE DOOR, TWO LOCKS

Think of it this way. There is a big, solid door, and on the other side of the door is success in selling. The door has two locks: a doorknob lock and a deadbolt. Each lock takes multiple keys to trip the tumblers and release the lock. Applying the keys of proper selling techniques lets us unlock the doorknob lock but not the deadbolt. Applying the keys of success lets us unlock the deadbolt but not the doorknob lock. Unless we have the keys to both selling AND success, we can't swing the door open and cross the threshold to achieve our goals and dreams in life.

I have discovered that this is true not just for selling but also for every endeavor in life. The keys of success are the same regardless of what we do. Unless we learn and apply the keys of success, all the doors to what we want in life will remain locked to us. However, applying the keys of success is not enough. We must also apply the keys to the task at hand.

Napoleon Hill, author of *Think and Grow Rich*, categorized these two separate skill sets as "general skills" and "specific skills." Specific skills are the knowledge and know-how necessary to perform a given task or trade. To become a professional golfer, for example, you have to learn how to expertly use all of the clubs in your bag and execute a variety of shots. General skills, on the other hand, are the personal, all-purpose skills needed to get the most out of your ability, get along with people, and get ahead in life.

These two skill sets are necessary to achieve everything in life. Most people, for example, would love to become financially wealthy. To do so, you must learn and apply the general keys of success AND the specific keys to financial prosperity. To be a good parent, you must apply the general keys to success AND the specific keys to good parenting. The same goes for your career, your health, your relationships, your marriage, whatever. If you want to become successful at anything, you must apply the general keys to success and the specific keys to whatever it is you're doing. That's what I mean when I say the door to success is one door, two locks.

This realization gave me a totally different view of what I needed to be teaching. As a professor, I was giving my students the keys to just one of the locks. I gave them the keys to selling but not to success. After leaving my class, the students who were somehow able to find the other keys on their own became successful. The ones who did not were out of luck. If I wanted my students to walk out of my class and through the door to successful selling, I needed to give them the keys to both success and selling.

MY STUDENTS BECAME MY TEACHERS

I faced a big problem. I knew how to teach selling. I had been doing that for years. But I didn't know how to teach success. I turned to my students for help. I set up a special topics class on success. I could structure the class any way I wanted to, so I simply told the students to find a book on success and read it. The only requirement was that they had to read something that would improve their life in some way. Then we would come to class and discuss what they were learning. Rather than me teaching them about success, we explored it together.

Many of the students told me that it was the best class they had ever taken. In fact, every single student rated the class with the highest marks they could on their faculty evaluations. For years, students in that class would come back to me telling me stories of how their lives changed because of what they learned in that one class. I'm not saying that I am such a great teacher. Remember, I didn't teach the class. The students did. The only difference between them and me is that I was drawing a salary and they had to pay tuition.

That semester was a turning point in my life. It changed the way I teach. Now, with a few exceptions and modifications, I bring this assignment into all my classes. I even developed a class called *Exploring Success,* where the whole class is built around the students selecting and reading self-improvement books.

STUDENTS CHANGE, THE KEYS DON'T

For years now, I have been going through this personal development exercise as part of all classes I teach. The exact nature of it changes a little based on the topical area I am teaching, but the reaction is always the same. Students love it. They become actively involved in the learning process. They come back, sometimes years later, and tell me how the things they learned totally changed their lives. Comments like Ashley's are very common. Again, I am not saying that I am a great teacher. I am not teaching. The students and I are just exploring together what it takes to be successful. It is what they learn on their own and what they teach each other that changes their lives.

I get a wide variety of students in my classes. A few of them are old enough to be my parents. Others are young enough to be my children. Some are rich. Others are poor. Some have never had a job. Others are already well established in their careers. They come from all races and backgrounds. They even come from all parts of the globe. Many of them are from the big city. Others are from farms and small communities. I get all different majors with all different aspirations in life.

The books they read are just as varied. Some books deal with specific problems like finding a job, getting over a broken relationship, dealing with eating problems, or overcoming social anxiety disorder. Many of them deal with relationship skills. Some of them deal with success in general. Biographies of successful people are also popular. I guess because I teach in the College of Business, a lot of my students like to read books on making money. Often students read books that help them in their spiritual lives. During our time together, we truly explore success from just about every imaginable perspective. Then we all come together and discuss what we are discovering.

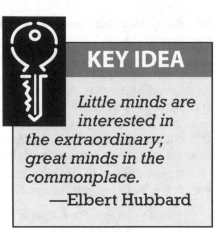

KEY IDEA

Little minds are interested in the extraordinary; great minds in the commonplace.

—Elbert Hubbard

By the end of the semester, the most amazing thing always happens. Despite the diversity of students, authors, and topics, a few key concepts always emerge as the basis for all success. Also, in any particular area of success, the same few keys always emerge. This happens every single time I teach. Students change and the books they read change. However, the keys to success that they discover are always the same. Here's the other thing I have noticed. The keys to success they discover aren't that difficult to understand. In fact, they are actually quite obvious.

THE FEW KEYS PARADIGM

Through my students, I discovered that there were a few simple keys to success. This pushed me to change my thinking. Having spent all of my adult life around university campuses, I thought that deeper means better. Professors often look down on that which is easy to understand. We tend to think that if everyone can grasp something, then it must not be worth knowing.

My students taught me that the keys to a better life aren't that complicated. Because of them, I eventually developed a huge appreciation for the simple truths of life. I also became very skeptical of the deeper mysteries of life. There are no secrets to success. Life isn't that complicated. Perhaps Elbert Hubbard was on to something when he said "Little minds are interested in the extraordinary; great minds in the commonplace."

I find this simple truth exciting. What it means is that the good life isn't reserved for the super-smart. We don't need a high IQ to achieve high levels of success. We simply need the ability to see and apply a few simple keys to success. As we will discover later in this book, it does require a high quality of thought to have a high quality of life. Fortunately, that quality of thought comes from mastering the few simple keys, not from uncovering a multitude of deep mysteries.

Now, I center all my teaching and all my life around the Few Keys Paradigm. Here is what it says.

The Few Keys Paradigm: There are a few universal keys to success that apply to everything we do. Also, each thing we do has its own unique set of keys. To have success in anything, we must identify and apply both sets of keys. We need to discover and apply the few universal keys of success and the few keys that are specific to whatever it is that we are doing.

Fortunately, these few keys are not that hard to discover.

Some people believe that the wisest person who ever lived was King Solomon. Listen to what he said about the wisdom it takes to succeed:

"Wisdom calls aloud from the streets. She raises her voice in the public square. At the head of the noisy street, she cries out. In the gateway to the city, she makes her speech. Does not Wisdom call out? Does not Understanding raise her voice? On the heights along the way, where the paths meet, she takes her stand. Beside the gates leading into the city, at the entrance, she cries aloud."

If I had a secret that I wanted to keep locked away, I certainly wouldn't rent the biggest billboard I could find on a crowded interstate highway and put it up there in huge bold letters. I certainly wouldn't take out a thirty-second spot during the Super Bowl and loudly proclaim it there.

KEY IDEA

To succeed, we must diligently seek the obvious.

But if we take Solomon's advice and fast-forward it to today, that is exactly where he is saying we can find wisdom. It isn't hidden away in some secret place staying quiet so we won't discover it. It's standing in the busiest place it can find, screaming at the top of its lungs.

Truth is, the secret of success isn't a secret at all. Truth is, it's open and obvious. So, if we want to succeed, we need to diligently seek the obvious. Does that seem ridiculous? If something is obvious, why should we need to diligently seek it? There are three reasons. If we don't seek the obvious, we will miss the obvious, we will forget the obvious, and we will avoid the obvious. Let's look at each of these individually.

Missing the Obvious

In the history of the world, there has never been an escape artist like the great Harry Houdini. It is said that he only had trouble escaping one time in his life. A new jail was built, and Houdini was challenged to free himself from one of the cells. He accepted the challenge. Though Houdini had never encountered a lock he could not pick, he was unable to get the door on this particular jail cell to click open. After wearing himself out trying, he finally collapsed against the door in total exhaustion. It swung open. The reason he had not been able to pick the lock was that the keeper of the jail played a trick on him. He never locked the door.

Houdini never made that mistake again. Before trying to escape, he started making sure the door was locked. Houdini learned to never overlook the obvious. Haven't we all made Houdini's mistake? Haven't we all tried to use our fancy skills to get through a door that wasn't even locked? At times, we all overlook the obvious.

Our tendency to overlook the obvious is actually quite intriguing. That's why we like riddles so much. They reveal just how easy it is to overlook the obvious. A good riddle has an answer that is obvious but not immediately apparent. Take the following riddle: A plumber in New Jersey has a brother who is an electrician in New York, but the electrician in New York doesn't have a brother who is a plumber in New Jersey. Why not? The answer to this riddle is both obvious and simple. However, not many of my students are able to get the answer right off the bat. (The answer is at the end of this section.)

That's the way it is with the keys to success. They are so simple, so obvious. The problem is that we trip all over the obvious. Once we finally discover the keys for ourselves, they make perfect sense. Unfortunately, it can take years of struggling before we figure them out.

Yet when we discover the keys to success, our lives can totally change. I had a student named Rodney come to me a few months after he took my class on success. He said he felt like he had lived his life in a cave. He said it was as if the class took him outside the cave and showed him a world he never knew existed. It's easy to see the trees, grass, birds, streams, sky, clouds, and all the other things that make this planet such a beautiful place to live. But he never saw them when he was back in the cave. He wanted to thank me for changing his life.

I thanked him, but then I told him that it wasn't me who changed his life. He changed his own life by venturing outside the cave. I didn't invent trees or grass. I didn't paint the sky blue or hang the clouds. I don't own the birds, and I didn't teach them to sing. In fact, I couldn't even figure out how to get out of my own cave on my own—I had to have my students help me find my way out.

I am just someone who wasted too many years in a dark, musty hole in the ground. Fortunately, I found a group of students who ventured outside of the cave with me. We found a beautiful world, and now I am looking for others who will take the trip with me. It's easy to move outside the cave, but it often takes someone who knows the route to show us how. Otherwise, we may spend our lives overlooking the obvious.

By the way, I am sure you didn't overlook the obvious, but in case you did, the electrician in New York has a *sister* who is a plumber in New Jersey.

FORGETTING THE OBVIOUS

Figuring out the obvious can happen quickly. Mastering the obvious takes much more time. In sports, there are a few keys to good form. Star athletes don't just learn them, they master them. The baseball player hits the same ball over and over. The golfer practices the same swing over and over. A basketball player shoots the same shot over and over. Every time they do, they drive the perfect movements deeper and deeper into their minds.

We shouldn't expect to master anything, even the simply keys to success, by hearing them once. We must constantly pound them deeper and deeper into our minds. We do this through hearing them over and over. I often read a good book several times. Each time, I better understand what the authors say. I am pounding the thoughts deeper and deeper into my mind. I read many different books on the same topic. I get different perspectives on the same topic. I am pounding the thoughts deeper and deeper into my brain.

Through repetition, we master something. We can never stop this process. We must be like the athletes who keep practicing the basics over and over. If they don't, they fall into bad habits. If we don't constantly keep feeding our minds the basic keys to success, we eventually start to forget them. The doors that had once been wide open to us begin slamming shut again.

KEY IDEA

Figuring out the obvious can happen quickly. Mastering the obvious takes much more time.

AVOIDING THE OBVIOUS

We may learn a key to success. We may even hear it over and over. That doesn't necessarily mean we will use it. All progress requires change, and most change is painful. We may avoid the obvious in an attempt to avoid the pain of change.

I have a friend named Jed who is in his late forties. He smokes like a chimney and drinks like a fish. He is seventy pounds overweight. He has no energy, and he is starting to experience some serious health problems. You don't have to go to medical school to figure out what Jed's problem is.

With just a few key changes, Jed's life could dramatically improve. He needs to quit smoking. He needs to quit drinking, or at least cut back dramatically. He needs to eat healthy food, and he needs to eat less of it. He needs to gradually increase his activity level until he can safely work his way into a sensible exercise program. Until he does these few key things, he will feel terrible. Unless he does them, he is headed for disaster.

Jed knows the keys to good health. He just doesn't want to pay the price to open the door. I don't want to minimize how difficult it would be for Jed. However, if he wants any reasonable quality of life, he must take these keys and act on them. Something has to motivate him to change.

We may hear something ninety-nine times and never change. Then on the hundredth time, we are profoundly impacted. It may be a story that made the idea hit home. It may be a different word or phrase that affects us. It might be the cumulative power of hearing it over and over that finally takes effect. It might be that we heard it at the exact right moment when we were emotionally ripe for change.

The more we hear something, even something we already know, the greater the chance we will be changed by it. We must always keep the ideas we want to adopt in front of us. They certainly can't affect us if they are stuffed away in a drawer someplace. If we keep the obvious in front of us, some day we may start doing the obvious things we need to do to have the life we want to have.

What Is Success?

So what is success? When you teach a class called *Exploring Success*, you need to have a definition of success. For a long time, I just borrowed others'. Earl Nightingale has a great one. "Success is the progressive realization of a worthy goal." I like that. For years, I used that definition.

Eventually, I came up with my own definition and here's what it is. *Success is having fun finding and fulfilling our purpose in life.* To be a success, we must find our purpose in life, we must fulfill it, and we must have some fun along the way.

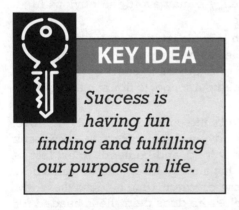

KEY IDEA

Success is having fun finding and fulfilling our purpose in life.

Fun is not the goal in life. Our goal should be to figure out why we're here and do what we were sent here to do. However, we haven't added much value to those around us if we are miserable in the process. The world has enough grumpy people. It doesn't need any more. When we enjoy life, we enrich the lives of everyone around us. When we walk around looking like we just finished off a case of lemons, we bring everyone around us down.

A student of mine named April recently shared with our class that her father died when she was twelve. He had been a supervisor at a factory that employed several thousand people. What she remembered most about him was that he always had an upbeat attitude. To him, life was fun. Because of that, everyone loved him. In fact, when he died, they built a memorial to him at the factory. April said she cherished the proud memory of her father because his upbeat spirit made such a big impact on so many people.

What legacy would April's father have left behind if he had been a gloomy wretch who always walked around with a scowl on his face? Would her father's company erect a monument so everyone could remember the grumpiest person to ever punch a clock? I don't think that April would have had a lot of people come up to her saying how much they missed her father's depressing moods. He would have died, and everyone would have been glad to stick his sad body in the ground.

The factory didn't hire April's father so that he could have a fun time down at the factory. His job was to make sure the factory kept churning out whatever it was churning out. That's why he was there. However, he was remembered for the fun he had doing so. We cannot talk about our journey to success and ignore the attitude we bring with us along the way.

Years ago, I read about an upbeat bus driver in a large city. When people got on his bus, he would greet them with great enthusiasm. As he drove the bus, he spoke with the passengers, joking with them and making an otherwise boring bus ride fun. When people got off his bus, he would send them on their way with some encouraging words. Here's what the author noticed. The passengers' dispositions would change in the few minutes they were on the bus. People who dragged themselves onto the bus would walk off with a bounce in their step.

The author asked a question. How many people do you think that bus driver had a positive impact on that day? A few hundred people got on his bus, and he seemed to uplift most of them. But he didn't just impact the people who got on the bus. All of the passengers also got off the bus. They went into offices, classrooms, and homes. Since they were more upbeat because of their bus ride, they probably uplifted a lot of other people along the way. In fact, just by having fun while he worked, this bus driver probably touched thousands of people every week.

FULFILLMENT IS FUN

The truly successful people are the ones who have fun while fulfilling their purpose in life. Actually, having fun in life is a lot easier if we are fulfilling a meaningful purpose. Perhaps the biggest barrier to enjoying life is that we never see a purpose for what we are doing.

One day, I was talking to an acquaintance of mine named Lance.

KEY IDEA

Having fun in life is a lot easier if we are fulfilling a meaningful purpose.

He was telling me how miserable he was. To him, life was totally useless. He wasn't even sure why he was alive.

Lance mentioned God, and so I asked him a question. "What was God thinking when He created you? Do you think he finished and said, 'Well, I don't know what I am supposed to do with that. Look at it. Useless! I hate it when I create someone without thinking what I am going to do with it. Well, I guess I will just plop him down on Earth and see what happens.' Is that what you think God said?"

Lance answered, "No, probably not."

"Absolutely not!" I replied emphatically. "Here is what God did. He had something specific he needed done. He said 'I know what I will do. I will create Lance to do it for me.' Then He made you exactly as He needed you to be to fulfill that purpose. He created you exactly as you are for a reason."

Lance thought for a moment and said, "Well, I don't know what that reason is."

"Of course you don't," I said. "That's why you are miserable. People who find their purpose in life and who are fulfilling it aren't miserable. You will stay miserable until you find your purpose in life. Quit cursing the one life God gave you. Start trying to figure out the reason He gave it to you in the first place."

I saw Lance a few weeks later, and his disposition had totally changed. He told me he was looking. "Looking for what?" I asked.

"The reason God put me on this Earth. I haven't found it yet, but I won't stop looking until I do. Knowing that makes life a lot easier to handle."

PURPOSE MAKES LIFE EXCITING

Lance discovered the difference between those who enjoy life and those who endure it. The difference is purpose. It is tempting to believe that what people want most in life is comfort. But that's not true.

What people want most from life is a purpose. If they can't find a purpose, they will settle for a life of ease. Sure, if we are going to live a meaningless life, it is better to live a comfortable meaningless life than an uncomfortable one. But we will sacrifice all our comforts in a heartbeat if there is a reason to do so. There isn't a person you or I know who wouldn't bolt out of his easy chair if it meant doing something meaningful with purpose.

Think about the military Special Forces. They will definitely call into question the hypothesis that "everyone is looking for an easy life." One of my students who had recently been in the Special Forces described for the class what it was like. For training, they starve you, freeze you, cook you, push you beyond physical exhaustion, deprive you of sleep, and do anything else they can think of to make your life miserable. They do that so that you will be prepared for the most dangerous of situations. When we go to war, the most likely ones to get killed or wounded are the members of these Special Forces.

Interesting job description, huh? One would think that it would be hard to find people to sign up for something like that. Not so. Only a small fraction of the applications for Special Forces are accepted. If everyone is seeking a life of ease, why are so many people trying to get into the hardest and most dangerous job on the planet?

Or what about athletics? I've taught at a couple schools with top-ranked NCAA sports programs. I have taught many all-star athletes,

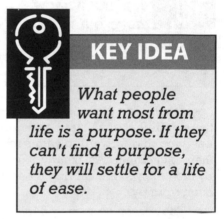

KEY IDEA

What people want most from life is a purpose. If they can't find a purpose, they will settle for a life of ease.

including several All-Americans. When they tell me what it takes to compete at that level, I am amazed. There is no comfort preparing to become a star athlete.

It is these athletes that kids idolize. How many kids dream of becoming a couch potato? How many kids come home from school and go straight for their dad's easy chair to imitate a life of ease? Around the country, are there a lot of aspiring young goof-offs dreaming of becoming the world's most comfortable person? I can just hear the announcer:

"Yes, folks, there he is. I think he's going for the potato chips. No, wait, he fakes for the chips and grabs the popcorn. Can he do it? Yes, he did it! He slammed down the popcorn and half a soft drink in one easy motion. This guy's incredible...." The point is that people do not want their lives to be a pursuit of ease or the absence of purpose. Even children aspire to a life of importance, not ease.

When we have a purpose, life is exciting. Life is fun. It gives us something to look forward to. It gives us a reason to get out of bed in the morning. Without it, life is a bore. We have nothing to look forward to in life. It is not what we have but what we have to look forward to that makes life exciting.

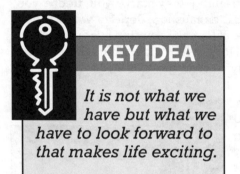

KEY IDEA

It is not what we have but what we have to look forward to that makes life exciting.

Think about children on Christmas morning. Before they open the presents, they are downright giddy. The child that you had to pry out of bed at 7:00 in the morning just a few days earlier is now using your bed as a trampoline at 5:00 a.m. Before they open the presents, they can barely contain themselves.

Finally, what they have been looking forward to arrives. They open their gifts. Now they have the goods. Now they can play with all the toys rather than stare at wrapped boxes. They have what they've been looking forward to with such great enthusiasm. What happens to their excitement? Amazingly, it goes away in a matter of minutes. In fact, by the time you are carving the turkey for Christmas lunch, the kids are often grumpy.

The reason so many people aren't enjoying life is that they don't have anything to look forward to. They are stuck on a road that is going nowhere. They look down the road, and all they see is more road just like the one they are already on. The only way their life will become exciting is to get on a different road, one that is going somewhere.

BUILDING A FUTURE, NOT WAITING ON IT

That doesn't mean we are waiting on the future. There is a big difference between building our future and waiting for it to arrive. When we are working on our future, life is great. When we are waiting on it, life becomes miserable.

I tell my students to remember back to junior high. Back then, we thought life would get great when? They always answer in unison. "High school." Then high school came. Life will be great when? "College." Okay, I say to them, now you're in college. Is life great or are you thinking that life will be great when you graduate and get a job?

Then I ask them this question. "If high school didn't make life great and college didn't make life great, do you really think life will be great when you get a job? If you aren't happy in college, you won't be happy when you get your job."

We get the job, and it isn't the key to happiness, so we think things will get good when we get married. Once married, we think having children will make life great. Then we think life will be great when the kids get out of diapers or go off to school. Then we think that life gets good when the kids can drive themselves around, or they are on their own. Finally, the children are gone and we think life will be great when we retire. Then what? Life will be great when we die?

Truth is, we don't have fun in life seeking fun. Just study history. Or look around you. The pleasure seekers have never been, nor will they ever be, the ones who really enjoy life.

We don't have fun by waiting on fun. If we are waiting on something to happen so that we can enjoy life, well, you can forget about that. If you are waiting on happiness, it will never get here. If we haven't found the secret to enjoying life where we are, we aren't going to find it somewhere else. The secret is in having a willing desire.

WILLING DESIRE

There is one idea that absolutely drives me nuts. I read it all the time in books. I hear it all the time from speakers. It is the idea that the key to happiness in life is to quit desiring anything. We are unhappy because we want more in life that what we have. The Quit Desiring theory says that our problems stem from our wanting more. So, if we learn to want less, the theory goes, then our problems go away.

Not so.

Despite what many people think, desire doesn't make us miserable. Even unfulfilled desire

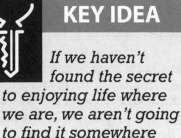

KEY IDEA

If we haven't found the secret to enjoying life where we are, we aren't going to find it somewhere else. The secret can be found in our desires.

isn't the problem. The problem is **unwilling desire**. We want something, but we are unwilling to do what it takes to get it. That makes us miserable. It's not the desire. It is the unwillingness to do everything needed to fulfill the desire.

Michelangelo was perhaps the greatest artist in the history of the world. How did he get there? Was it by being satisfied with what he had? Absolutely not. Here is what Michelangelo prayed. "Lord, grant that I may always desire more than I can achieve." There is incredible wisdom in that prayer.

KEY IDEA

Happy is the one who dreams big dreams and is willing to pay the price to make them happen.

Conventional wisdom says that success occurs when we achieve all we desire. Actually, that is the point where failure occurs. Thomas Edison said, "Show me a totally satisfied person, and I will show you a total failure." Why? It is desire that gets us up in the morning. It is desire that makes us work hard all day. It is desire that makes us willing to get better and do more than we have ever done before.

Someone once asked John D. Rockefeller what was the most rewarding million he ever made. He said, "The next." Rockefeller had more money than he could ever spend, but he wasn't deriving his enjoyment from all he had. He got enjoyment from what he wanted rather than what he had.

There are two ways to be miserable and only one way to enjoy life. One way to be miserable is to not want anything. If we don't have desire, we don't sit around totally satisfied. We sit around totally bored. We sit around totally useless.

Another way to be miserable is to have desire but be unwilling to do what it takes to reach that desire. That type of desire doesn't make us enjoy life. It makes us frustrated. Lacking desire causes boredom. Unwilling desire causes frustration.

The only way to enjoy life is to have a willing desire. When I was a teenager, I had a poster on the wall of my room that had a profound impact on me. It said "Happy is the man who dreams dreams and is willing to pay the price to make them happen." If we want to enjoy life, we must have desires and we must be willing to do what it takes to fulfill those desires.

What does it take to fulfill our desires? We must be willing to work. We must be willing to risk. We must be willing to delay pleasure. We must be willing to endure pain. If the desire is big enough, most people are willing to do all these things.

KEY IDEA

Growth isn't a key to success. It's the door.

WHAT IS THE DOOR TO SUCCESS?

There is one thing that we must do to achieve our desires that few of us are willing to do. We must be willing to change. The real pain in desire isn't that I want something and I don't have it. The real pain in desire comes from the fact that I want something and yet I am unwilling to change to get it.

A major theme of this book is growth. It will be discussed in every chapter. Growth isn't a key to success. It's the door. If we can have everything we want with who we are, we don't want enough. As we grow, we will change into the person we must become to achieve whatever it is that we want to achieve. We will grow in knowledge. We will grow in wisdom. We will grow in understanding.

What will happen when we grow? When we grow, we will be able to have more, do more things, go more places, and see more sights. Life will be exciting because we will see the road we are on, and we will enjoy the journey more. Our relationships will improve. Our finances will get better. By wanting more and being willing to change to get more, our life will improve.

As we grow, our thinking changes. That's a huge change because all success comes through correct thinking. The first key to success reveals how important it is to judge our thinking based on where it is getting us. So let's start exploring the first key to all success.

KEY 1

Action is the blossom of thought,
and joy and suffering are its fruits.
—James Allen, from *As a Man Thinketh*

DISCERNMENT: JUDGE THE SEED BY THE HARVEST

It's pretty easy to figure out what type of seed a farmer planted. All we need to do is show up around harvest time. If he planted wheat, we will see "amber waves of grain." If he planted cotton, we will see snow white balls of cotton. If he planted corn, we will find stalks of corn.

It doesn't take a Ph.D. to figure this stuff out. All it takes is a knowledge of the most basic law of life. A farmer reaps what he sows. Even a city kid who has never been to a farm knows that.

There is more to farming than simply planting the right kind of seed. Farmers must fertilize and irrigate. They must get rid of the weeds and keep the pests away. A good farmer applying the proper farming techniques can yield a much bigger crop than one who simply tosses seed out and hopes all will turn out well.

However, there is one thing no farmer can do. Once he has planted the seed, he can't change the crop. Even the best fertilizer and irrigation can't grow corn from cotton seed. In fact, this is one of the big frustrations of farming. If cotton is in the ground, the farmer is going to market with cotton. The price of cotton may tumble and the price of corn may head for the sky, but, come harvest time, the farmer will be selling cotton, not corn. A great farmer can be in trouble if he chooses the wrong seed. Even a mediocre farmer can do well if he happens to pick the right seed. That's because in farming everything grows from the seed.

OUR THOUGHTS ARE OUR SEEDS

Everything we have in life comes from what we do, and everything we do comes from how we think. Thus, the seeds of our life are our thoughts. Just as the farmer has no choice over the crop once he has

KEY IDEA

The seeds of our life are our thoughts. We have no choice over what our life produces once we have chosen our thoughts.

chosen the seed, we have no choice over what our life produces once we have chosen our thoughts. Other things may have some impact on how much we produce, but nothing has as big of an impact on our life as the way we think.

Any study of successful people reveals an amazing ability that people have to overcome almost anything. People can always rise above circumstances. They do it all the time. Physical disabilities can't keep a person down. Hardships and failures are commonplace among the overachievers of the world. We can rise above almost anything. In fact, there is only one thing we cannot rise above. That one thing is the quality of our thought. Nothing in life can keep us down but our own thinking.

This is the most basic of all keys to success. If we want a high quality of life, we must have a high quality of thought. The way to have a better life is to improve the quality of our thinking. How we think has given us what we have. The seeds of our thinking determine our actions, and our actions determine our results.

Ms. Crab and Gertrude

Several semesters ago, I had a student named Monica. She always wore a smile and had a wonderful attitude. That's why I was surprised when she came to class one day and wasn't her usual bright self. It didn't take long before Monica shared with the class what was bothering her. She told us that she worked with an older woman who was constantly criticizing her. I don't remember this coworker's name, so, for reasons that will become apparent later in the chapter, I will just call her Ms. Crab.

Ms. Crab holds a master's degree and yet the best job she could get was one that anyone off the street could do. She felt overqualified and underpaid. As a result, she had a real big chip on her shoulder.

That morning, right before class, Ms. Crab let loose on Monica. "They really have you fooled," Ms. Crab said flatly. "You come in here and rush around all day long. For what? The measly wages these cheap people pay you? I don't understand why you think you have to solve the problems of every whining customer that comes in that door. I don't understand why you think you have to work so hard. You won't find me doing that, not for what they pay us."

Monica asked me how she should handle Ms. Crab.

"It depends," I said.

"Depends on what?" Monica asked.

"It depends on where you want to be in ten years. Do you want to finish school, get a master's degree, work for ten years, and still not be any further in life than you are right now? If so, then I would pay very close attention to everything Ms. Crab says. She seems to have figured out quite well how to commit career suicide. If that's what you want, then I would certainly listen to her."

"Come on," Monica said, "You know that's not what I want."

"Then don't get mad at Ms. Crab," I said. "She is just stating the obvious."

Monica was totally surprised. "What do you mean she is stating the obvious? Do you agree with her?"

"Absolutely, I agree with her 100%. She says she doesn't understand why you do all the things you do to make your store a better place. Of course she doesn't understand. If she understood why you do what you do, then she would do it, too. She wouldn't be stuck going nowhere and she wouldn't be walking around with such a big chip on her shoulder. The fact that she isn't solving her problem proves that she doesn't understand. I agree with her. She doesn't understand."

KEY IDEA

Nothing in life can keep us down except our own thinking.

I reminded Monica of the most basic principle that is foundational to all success. We are where we are in life because of the way we think. To drive home this point, I shared an experience my wife, Lisa, and I had just that morning. As I do with almost all my writing, teaching, and speaking, I wanted to use a fictitious name. I asked my class to give me a name.

An ex-marine in back of the class yelled out, "Gertrude."

"Gertrude it is," I replied. I then proceeded to tell my class the story of Gertrude.

Gertrude burst into our life Thanksgiving week. My wife called me and told me that an acquaintance of hers didn't have anything to eat for Thanksgiving. Initially, I thought that just meant that she did not have turkey and dressing. I was wrong. It literally meant that there was not one thing for her family to eat in their whole house, and they had no way of getting any money for the next two weeks.

I didn't want to see Gertrude and her family starve, but I also believe that people should, if possible, earn their money. So I told Lisa to pick some things that she thought Gertrude could do from her "honey-do" list and tell her that, if she wanted to do them, I would pay her when I got home.

KEY IDEA

If we want a high quality of life, we must have a high quality of thought.

Gertrude eagerly agreed. She did a great job, so we continued having her come and work around our house. For the next few months, Gertrude was over working on our house every day. She remodeled our bathrooms. She painted the outside of our house. She shampooed the carpets. She replaced windows. She was able to put food in her cabinets and keep her dignity, and I was able to opt out of working around the house without even feeling guilty.

Since Gertrude spent so much time over at our house, we got a very good picture of what her life was like. It was a total mess. It wasn't just her finances where she had problems. The most common words I heard out of her son's mouth were "I hate you, Mom." She wasn't 100% sure her husband was the boy's father. Her marriage was in shambles. We pleaded with her to go to the local battered women's home for protection when she told us that her husband had threatened her with a chain saw. She cried all the time. She didn't feel like she had any friends. She was estranged from her parents and her brother. It was hard to find any aspect of her life that wasn't a total wreck.

Gertrude also got a good chance to see how we lived our lives from the inside. She was absolutely amazed that anyone lived as we do. Over and over, Gertrude told Lisa and me that we live in a "fairy-tale world." Our kids love us. We have a great marriage. We don't have any financial stress or strain. Both Lisa and I love what we do. Our parents, brothers, and sisters all like us. We are in good health. Gertrude told us that everything she wanted in life, we have.

The strange thing was that Gertrude, while envying our product, constantly criticized our process. She envied our children but criticized our child raising. She envied our finances but criticized the way we handled our money. She envied the love Lisa and I had for each other but constantly criticized the dynamics of our relationship.

One evening, Lisa had several friends over for a get-together. Gertrude was one of the guests. Men and children weren't invited, so I stayed with the kids in another part of the house. I went to bed before the party was over so I didn't talk with Lisa about her party until the next morning. When I did, she looked as though she hadn't slept all night. I asked, "How did things go last night?"

"It was 90% great and 10% terrible," she answered.

"I bet I can guess the 10%," I said. "Gertrude, right?"

She nodded yes. "I couldn't sleep last night for thinking of all the terrible things Gertrude said."

"What did she say?" I asked.

"She spent the whole night criticizing me. She told everyone at the party how she thought everything I do is wrong." By this time Lisa was almost in tears.

"And that bothers you?" I asked, sounding a bit surprised.

"Of course it bothered me," she said. "Wouldn't it bother you if somebody criticized everything about your life right there in front of your friends?"

"Not if it were Gertrude," I chuckled. "Do you know why she criticizes you? It's because Gertrude and you think differently. If you thought the way she did, she wouldn't have anything to criticize you about. You would have spent the whole evening agreeing about how to raise kids, spend money, treat family, and the like. Just remember, when Gertrude criticizes you, she is stating the obvious. She thinks differently than you. But she doesn't even have to open her mouth for you to know that."

"Why's that?" Lisa asked.

"We are where we are in life because of the way we think. The way you think has given you this 'fairy-tale world' Gertrude talks about. The way Gertrude thinks has given her the nightmares she is constantly crying about. If Gertrude thought like you, she would have what you

KEY IDEA

*We are where
we are in life
because of the way
we think.*

have. If you thought like her, you would have what she has. Your lives are as different as night and day. That means you and she must think differently from each other."

I continued. "That should only bother you if you want what Gertrude has. So tell me, exactly what part of her life do you want? Do you want me to bring the kids in here and have them scream 'I hate you'? Do you want me to clean out the bank accounts and empty the kitchen cabinets so that we can starve for a few days? What do you want me to do? Do you want me to go get the chain saw? Specifically, which part of Gertrude's life do you want?"

"I don't want any part of her life!" Lisa responded emphatically.

"Then, I guess it doesn't matter that she criticized you. I guess it doesn't matter that you and she think differently. Be glad that you do."

I saw the frustration totally drain from Lisa's face. "I wish I would have woken you up last night, and we would have had this conversation then. I wouldn't have spent the night tossing and turning, worrying about what Gertrude said."

THE REAL SOURCE OF OUR PROBLEMS

I have seen people point to someone like Gertrude or Ms. Crab and flippantly say, "She just wants to be unhappy." Not so. Nobody wants to be miserable. Gertrude wants to be happy. So does Ms. Crab. If they really knew what they would have to do to be happy, they would do it. Their problem is that neither of them understands why they are where they are in life.

If you were to ask Ms. Crab for the reasons for her career struggles, I am sure she would have many answers to give you. She would blame the economy. She would blame her boss. She would blame all the other employers on this planet who don't give her the job she wants. She would blame her college for not preparing her for the real world. She would blame the government. She would blame it on the fact that she's a woman. She would blame it on the fact that she's too pretty or not pretty enough. I am sure she would tell you she is either too light complexioned or too dark complexioned. There would be no shortage of reasons Ms. Crab could give us for her career going nowhere.

What Ms. Crab fails to realize is that, all around her, people are moving on in their careers. These people have bosses that are just like hers. They must face the same employment interviews she does. They went to the same college she did. Many of them are women. Some of them are pretty. Some of them are not. They come from all races. In fact, you could take any excuse Ms. Crab could come up with, and it would be easy to find many people moving on in their career who face the very same challenge. What we couldn't find is someone who has the same mind-set as Ms. Crab who is moving on in her career.

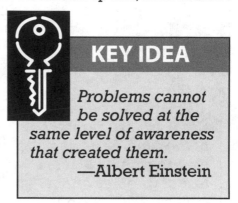

KEY IDEA

Problems cannot be solved at the same level of awareness that created them.
— Albert Einstein

Ms. Crab's real problem is that she missed the first key to opening the door to success. We are where we are in life because of the way we think. The same could be said of Gertrude. From the few months she spent fixing up our house, I could write a book on why her thinking won't get her what she wants in life. Still, she was absolutely oblivious to the fact that her problems can be traced to the way she thinks. If Gertrude and Ms. Crab ever want to improve their lives, they must improve their thinking.

The same could be said of us all. Albert Einstein once observed that the problems we face can't be solved with the same thinking that created them. Our level of thinking brought us to where we are. The same level of thinking can't possibly take us any further.

If we want a better marriage, we don't need a new husband or wife. We need to improve our level of thinking about how we treat our husband or wife. If we want better children, we can't trade ours in for the kids next door. We must improve how we think about parenting. If we want more money, our financial thinking must improve. If we want better health, we can't run out and buy another body. Something needs to change in the way we think about physical fitness. If we keep thinking as we are thinking, then we will keep doing what we are doing and we will keep getting what we are getting. To change your life, the first thing you have to do is change your thinking.

HOW TO JUDGE OUR THINKING

There is always room to improve our lives, so there is always the need to improve our thinking. Unfortunately, few of us feel the need to improve our thinking, and here's why. We all think we are right all of the time.

Have you ever heard someone say, "He always thinks he is right." That statement could apply to us all. We all believe we are right all the time; thus, none of us see the need to change our thinking. If I believe something, I believe it is right. If I didn't believe it was right, I wouldn't believe it. As soon as I discover I am wrong, I change what I believe. When I do, I quickly go back to believing I am right. To believe anything whatsoever means we believe we are right.

KEY IDEA

We all believe we are right all of the time. Believing we are right is a poor test of whether or not we actually are right.

That's why believing that we are right is such a pitiful poor way to judge whether or not we actually are right. As Jim Rohn says, "Sincerity is not a test of truth." We must find a better way to evaluate our thinking than whether or not we think we are right.

Let me propose a better standard. It is based on the Law of the Harvest: We reap what we sow. Since the seeds of life are our thoughts, we can then judge our thinking by what we are getting in life. That's the first key to all success. We judge the seed by the harvest. We judge our thoughts by our lives.

If harvest time comes and we have corn, we shouldn't pretend we planted wheat. If we are broke, we shouldn't say, "But I know I planted the seeds of wealth." If all we have is hatred and discord in our life, let's quit thinking we planted seeds of love. If we are overweight and out of shape, let's not fool ourselves into thinking that this harvest came from planting seeds of good health. If we don't like the harvest, let's not blame the crop. Instead, let's look for new seed. The real test of our thinking is to look at where we are in life. Our thinking can't be all right if our life is all wrong.

Now that doesn't mean that everything we have is what we planted. Even farmers have things in their fields that they didn't plant. They call them weeds. Even the field planted with the best of seeds must be weeded or the good crop will be choked out. Our lives must be weeded, too. We must pull out by the roots everything in our life that is not what we want to harvest. However, if we finish pulling weeds and all we have left is an empty field, we must re-evaluate the seed.

KEY IDEA

Our thinking can't be all right if our life is all wrong. We must put all of our thinking to the test of life.

So the ultimate test of our thinking is not whether we can convince ourselves that we are right. I am not the test of truth and neither are you. Life is the test of truth. We must subject all of our thinking to the test of life. We must judge the seed by the harvest.

IT'S NOT A MATTER OF INTELLIGENCE

Since neither Gertrude nor Ms. Crab is reaping the harvest they want, it is clear that they need to sow different seeds. They need to change the way they think. Until they do their lives won't change. Am I saying that Gertrude is not intelligent? Absolutely not. I could tell by being around her that she is actually an extremely intelligent person. Ms. Crab is probably pretty smart, too. It takes some brains to earn a master's degree.

Broken thinking is seldom a problem of low intelligence. It is almost always a problem of being given the wrong information. We don't necessarily believe something because it is true. We believe something because we have heard it over and over. Even a lie, if told repeatedly, will be received by our minds as truth.

Early in his speaking career, Zig Ziglar heard a speaker say, "You are where you are in life because that is exactly where you want to be." Well, that made sense to Ziglar. He traveled around proclaiming to audiences everywhere that they where exactly where they wanted to be.

Then one night he finished speaking in Birmingham, Alabama. The next morning, he had an early speaking engagement in Meridian,

Mississippi. As he drove from Birmingham to Meridian, he ran into some construction detours. He stopped for directions. He followed the directions to the letter only to find that they took him in the exact wrong direction.

An hour later, he sat there, many miles further away from Meridian than he was when he stopped to get the directions. That's when he realized something. He wasn't there because that was where he wanted to be. He wanted to be asleep in a soft bed in Meridian. Never again did Ziglar tell people that they were where they were in life because it was where they wanted to be.

Zig Ziglar is a very intelligent man. He didn't go the wrong way because he was stupid. He went the wrong way because someone gave him the wrong directions. I know many very intelligent people whose thinking is taking them in the wrong direction. Their problem is not a lack of smarts. Their problem is that their minds have been fed the wrong information. No matter how wrong a piece of information is, we will believe it if we hear it over and over.

KEY IDEA

The good life isn't reserved for the super-smart. We simply need to be careful about what we feed our minds.

I find that exciting, and here's why. It means the good life isn't reserved for the super-smart. We all have access to the thoughts we need to succeed. We simply need to be careful about what we feed our minds.

There are four major influences on how we think. They are the people we associate with, the books we read, the entertainment we watch and hear, and the dialog that goes on within our heads. We can greatly improve our lives by choosing these four influences wisely. Let's explore each.

THE PEOPLE WE ASSOCIATE WITH

The biggest influence on the way we think is the people we are around. We all know what a big effect peer pressure can have on children and teenagers. Say a teenage boy has been a great student, never getting in trouble, making good grades, showing respect for adults, and the like. Then he suddenly changes. He starts smoking and drinking. His grades drop. He starts using bad language and talking back to his parents and teachers. If you were to ask his parents what happened, most of the time they would say that the young man "fell into a bad crowd." We all know that teens are incredibly susceptible to taking on the attitudes, beliefs, and behaviors of those around them.

When does that change? When do we stop being strongly influenced by those around us? At twenty, thirty, or forty? Not at all. We stop being influenced by those around us when we die. Until then, we will be like the people we surround ourselves with.

For that reason, we must look very closely at the people we choose to be around. Are they the type of people we want to become? If not, then we must find a way to get around the people who are. As corny as it sounds, you really can't soar with the eagles when you are surrounded by turkeys.

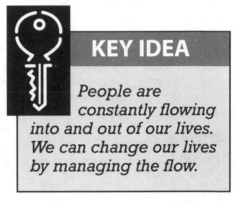

KEY IDEA

People are constantly flowing into and out of our lives. We can change our lives by managing the flow.

That doesn't mean we suddenly change all our associations in life. That's not even possible. I am not suggesting that you call up Mom and say, "Sorry, I can't see you any more. You are bringing me down." Due to work commitments and family ties, there are some people we can't avoid. On the other hand, we all have some discretion over the people we are around.

People are constantly flowing into and out of our lives. We can change the people in our lives by simply managing this flow. The challenge is to make sure that we associate with people by choice and not by chance. Chance is against us, and here's why. The people we need to learn from aren't looking for us. On the other hand, those who could prove hazardous to our thinking are seeking us out.

Whenever we accept a new job, we can expect a visit. Someone will pull us aside and proceed to tell us "how things work around here." Have you ever noticed who that person is? Is it the person who started out as the janitorial assistant to the mail room trainee and worked his way up to senior vice president? No, it's the person who started at the bottom of the corporate food chain twenty years ago and has been moving down ever since. The person who wants to tell us "how things work around here" is clueless. He has no idea how things work.

The ones who really know how things work are too busy working to take the time to seek out every new soul and tell them how to get where they are. They are willing to talk to us, but we must go to them. I am not suggesting that we should be stuck-up snobs. We shouldn't walk around thinking we are "too good" for others. Recently, I had a student ask me if we should ever spend time with people who aren't where we want to be.

"Absolutely, we should do just that," I replied. "In fact, our greatest rewards in life will not come from those who help us but from those we help. One of the big rewards of improving ourselves is that we can help others with what we've learned. If others are seeking our help to figure out how they can get better, then, indeed, we should be there for them. However, there are a lot of people who are doing just the opposite. They are grabbing onto us to bring us down. Those are the ones we should avoid like the plague."

KEY IDEA

Even a lie, if we hear it enough times, will be accepted by our minds as true.

I then went on to tell the class how you hunt for crabs. You walk down the beach with a bucket in hand. When you catch a crab, you toss him into your bucket. At that point, you had better keep your eye on him because he can scale the side of the bucket and be gone faster than you can say crab soufflé. So, with one eye on the bucket and the other on the beach, you look for your second crab. Once you get crab number two in the bucket, your worries are over. If one crab tries to climb the bucket wall, the other one will yank him back down. They could easily march out of your bucket single file, but they won't. They would rather cook together than cooperate so they both could escape.

We can't afford to let crabs into our life. When we start to climb, they reach up and yank us back down. They don't pull us down with their claws. They do so with words and ideas. They say things like "You know you can't do that. They won't let you. The system is fixed. You can't get anywhere in life. What makes you think you can escape. We are all stuck."

If you listen to enough of that thinking, you will begin believing it.

None of it is true, but remember, even a lie, if told to us enough times, will begin to be accepted by our minds as truth.

When we choose the people we are around, we choose our thoughts. When we choose our thoughts, we choose the life we will live. That's why we must choose our associates based on what kind of life we want to live.

THE BOOKS WE READ

The most important thing I can do to help my students succeed is to get them into the habit of reading good books. Most of them have already filled their minds with thousand upon thousands of hours of television. Daily, they hear the same songs over and over until the lyrics are pounded into their brains. Very little of what they watch or hear will get them where they want to be. In fact, a lot of it is taking them in the exact wrong direction.

My primary goal is not to give them ideas but to teach them a habit. I force them to read personal development books every day all semester long. I am hoping that they form a habit and it sticks. If they continue doing so after they leave my class, I will have succeeded. If they do not, I have failed. I don't judge my success as a professor by what my students learn, what grades they make, or how they appraise the course. I evaluate my effectiveness solely based on the number of students who continue the personal development process after they have left my class.

Here's why. I know that the quality of my students' lives will be determined by the quality of their thinking. In one semester, their thinking can start moving in a positive direction. However, it will not keep moving in the right direction unless something pushes it that way. For growth to continue, they must continue to read the things that will make them grow. The best place to find such material is in quality personal development books.

At the start of the semester, many of my students are hesitant to read this kind of books. They think "I don't need self-help books. My self doesn't need any help." Some of them have this notion that only people with messed-up lives need to read personal development books. Fortunately, by the end of the semester, they realize the flaw in their logic. You don't have to be messed up to try to improve yourself.

They discover that it is just the opposite. People who read these books have fewer problems than those who don't. Why? People who read personal development books learn the truths to a better life. People who miss the books miss those truths. It is just like everything else in life. What you work at is what you get good at. What you ignore goes the other way.

Take a trip through your neighborhood and look at the yards. Take note of the ones that really need some work and the ones that don't. Then drive through it again on Saturday. Where are you going to find people doing yard work? They won't be in the ugly yards. The people with the beautiful yards are the ones working hard on their yards. That is why they have beautiful yards. The people whose yards really need work are nowhere to be found. Their yards need work but they aren't working in them. That's why they need work.

Go to the local gym at 5:30 in the morning. See what kind of people are there. It's the people who are already in good shape. The people who really need to be there are still snoozing away in bed. The people who are in good shape are working out. That's why they are in good shape.

I teach leadership seminars. Guess who shows up at them. It's not the people who really need to develop their leadership skills. It is the people who are already good leaders. They are the ones looking for even better ways to lead. The guy who couldn't lead an ant to sugar isn't there. He will tell you, "I don't need that leadership development stuff. I'm okay as I am."

I have heard people say that only losers read that personal development stuff. Who makes that kind of statement? It is never a person who has his life in order. It is always a person who desperately needs the insights such books can provide. When I hear someone say that, I feel somewhat like the woman on the elevator. The doors open and a man gets on. He brings with him a terrible body odor. She wants to politely tell him that he needs to take care of it and so she says. "One of our deodorants is not working."

He replies, "It's not mine. I'm not wearing any."

The people who read personal development books are developing. They are building a better life. That's why, if you walk into the house

KEY IDEA

The people who are reading personal development books are developing.

of a highly successful person, the first thing you are likely to notice is a large, well-stocked library. If you walk into the houses of people living well below their potential, you will likely find the biggest entertainment center money can buy. Everything in the living room will be centered around it.

It isn't that the successful person can afford the library, but all the struggling person can afford is an entertainment center. Those who are living the good life got there by feeding their minds positive things. Those who are struggling will continue to do so until they start learning the ideas so readily available in good books. Mark Twain said it best: "The person who won't read is no better off than the person who can't read." Amen to that.

THE ENTERTAINMENT WE SEE AND HEAR

This doesn't mean we shouldn't watch TV or listen to music. The entertainment industry is huge. It is diverse. There are some really powerful positive things out there. On the other hand, there's also some real trash that will totally mess up how we think. We must make sure that our entertainment is enhancing rather than undermining our quest to develop useful thinking.

KEY IDEA

As we are being entertained, we are driving ideas deep into our minds.

We often underestimate the powerful impact that entertainment can have on our thinking. When we want to be entertained, we can watch television, go to the movies, or listen to music. We are fortunate that we have so much to choose from in these three areas. However, as we make our choices, here's what we must remember. As we are being entertained, we are also driving ideas and beliefs deep into our brains.

When the TV or stereo goes on, our minds don't stop accepting information. It still uses the information it is receiving to form beliefs. Anytime we are giving information to our brains, it is changing the way we think. Knowing that, we should pick our entertainment with care.

When I tell my students that TV, music, or movies can change us, I am usually met with skepticism. To make my point, all I need to do is point out how powerful advertising is. In the United States alone, hundreds of billions of dollars is spent buying little fifteen-second and thirty-second advertising spots. Either these short, brief spots change people's behavior, or all these brilliant captains of industry who bought them have been duped. If short little advertising spots don't change people's behavior, the smartest business people in the world are wasting billions upon billions of dollars every year.

These advertisers aren't wrong. Even short commercials can change our behavior. If so, imagine how much of an impact four hours a night of television can have on us. How about a three-minute song played over and over until we will still remember every single word thirty years from now. What about a ninety-minute movie that has the power to move us to tears? The entertainment we see and hear does have an impact, and we only harm our thinking if we act as if it doesn't.

THE DIALOG THAT GOES ON IN OUR HEADS

The other big impact on our thinking is our internal dialog. Some people think you are crazy if you talk to yourself. Actually, something is wrong if you don't. We all have this dialog going on in our head all the time. We just don't let it slip out through our mouth so others can hear what's being said.

A Native American elder one time spoke of the dialog that was going on within his mind. "It is as if I have two dogs within me constantly fighting. One dog is good and pure. The other is evil and ugly. They are constantly fighting day and night." Someone asked him which one usually wins. The man thought for a moment and then replied, "The one I feed."

Our goal is to take control of that dialog. We must make sure that we are feeding the dog we want to win. We must be careful what we say to ourselves because if we say it over and over, we will believe it. I say it again. Even a lie, if it is said over and over will be believed by our minds.

For example, have you ever said to yourself, "I can't remember names." As long as you keep telling yourself that, you will never get good at remembering names. Your brain doesn't take that statement as an observation. It takes it as a command: "Forget names."

So what do we do? Should we tell ourselves, "I am great at remembering names" when we are not? Should we "fake it 'til we make it," as some suggest? No, here's what we should do. Read memory books and learn how to better remember names. Practice remembering names.

When we do, we have something to tell our minds. "I am getting better at remembering names."

As we affirm over and over in our mind where we are going, not where we are, our minds begin to take us there. On the other hand, if we are constantly harping on where we don't want to be, our minds will take us there. We choose where we are going by choosing what we say to ourselves.

KEY IDEA

As we affirm over and over in our minds where we want to be, not where we are, our minds begin to take us there.

THOU SHALL NOT FOOL THYSELF

If we feed our minds the right things, we can get what we want from life. There are thoughts out there that, if we embrace them, will give us almost anything we may want from life. We must find them and feed them to our minds. If the thoughts we have aren't giving us what we want, it's time to put our minds on a new diet and improve what we are feeding it. We may fool ourselves, but we can't fool life. Life will reward us or punish us based on the quality of our thinking.

John Sheppard is a missionary to Africa. He tells a story that happened when he was a child. He lived on a farm. It was Monday, and the circus was coming to town the next weekend. He and his brothers wanted to go, but it was the season for planting. His father told the boys that they could go if they planted a field by Friday night.

They planted most of the field, but they realized they wouldn't get the job done in time for the circus. So, instead of planting the last two rows, they just dumped the seed in a nearby rotted-out stump. They told their father that they had planted the whole field and so he let them go to the circus.

Their little stunt worked fine as long at the seed was in the ground. Unfortunately for the boys, seeds grow. A few weeks later, there were two empty rows with nothing growing. Nearby, there was a tree trunk looking good for the harvest. Needless to say, Sheppard's father was quite upset with his boys, and he expressed his displeasure in no uncertain terms. The trip to the circus was not worth the punishment they received for dumping the seed.

Sheppard learned an important lesson. We can mess up the planting and no one will know the difference while the seed is in the ground. Inevitably, though, the seed will grow and the truth will be revealed. We can fool others for a while. We can even fool ourselves. But we can't fool the Law of the Harvest.

KEY IDEA

Nature delights in punishing stupid people.
—Emerson

We are all planting seeds of thought that will grow into actions. Those actions will turn into a harvest. We will reap what we sow. Good or bad, we will reap much more than we sow. Because we reap later than we sow, we can fool ourselves for a while. But, come harvest time, if I have an empty field and a happy tree stump, I can't blame the field or the stump. I have to look at the person who planted the seed. I can find that person in the mirror.

For several years, I have had this poster hanging in my office. It shows some grain growing and it simply says "Thou shall not fool thyself." It is there to remind me of the first key to success. I must always be willing to put my thinking to the test. I can't judge my thinking by whether or not I think I am right. I must always submit my thinking to the test of life. In those areas where I want a higher quality of life, I know I must develop a higher quality of thought.

To be honest, I don't like being so brutal in judging my thoughts. I like thinking I am right. I don't like changing the way I think. I would much rather go along pretending everything is fine. I am right, the world is wrong. That would be nice except for the fact that the world won't bend to my thinking.

Emerson said it so well when he observed, "Nature delights in punishing stupid people." It is painful subjecting all my thinking to the Law of the Harvest. However, as I have learned the hard way many times, it is much more painful being "nature's delight."

KEY 2

A pessimist sees the difficulty in every opportunity;
an optimist sees the opportunity in every difficulty.
—Winston Churchill

OPTIMISM: BE REALISTIC, SEE WHAT CAN BE

Optimism is at the root of all successful thinking. If we believe we can accomplish great things, we can. If we think we are destined for a life of mediocrity, that is all we will achieve. Henry Ford was indeed correct when he said, "If you think you can or you think you can't, you're right."

Unfortunately, we live in a world where pessimists massively outnumber optimists. Of course, none of us believe we are pessimistic. The most negative person you can find will tell you, "I'm not being pessimistic. I'm just being realistic." Ask a pessimist and he will say, "I just call it as I see it." That's the problem. The irony is that, because pessimists can't see beyond what they can see, they are totally unrealistic.

The pessimist sees what is and assumes that's all there could ever be. The optimist realizes that things can always get better. When the pessimist tells us to be realistic, he is in essence telling us to limit our vision to what we can see. We only see a small fraction of what can be. Pessimists let their sight limit their reality. Optimists let their vision become their reality. The optimist simply sees reality before it arrives. That's why optimism is always more realistic than pessimism.

THE REALITY WE HAVE CREATED

The reality we have today is here because some very optimistic people did some incredible things while ignoring a chorus of pessimists singing, "it can't be done." So many things that we accept as commonplace today were deemed impossible just a short time back in history.

Imagine what would happen if someone from the nineteenth

century was miraculously transmitted to modern-day America. He would be in for a big surprise. The first thing he might see is me talking on my cell phone. He can't understand why I am standing there all by myself talking to my hand. With a strange look on his face, he asks me what I am doing.

I show him my cell phone and say that I am talking to my father. He looks at the little box in my hand and replies, "Your father must be real small to fit in that little thing."

"My father's not inside this phone," I say. "He's in California."

That doesn't clarify much for my time traveler. My father's not in this little box. He's all the way across the country, and I am talking to him? I can see that I need to explain cell phones. "See, my voice is sent from this box to a tower a few miles away. From there, it is beamed into outer space, where it is bounced off a ship floating around up there. It zooms back down to Earth across the country, where another tower sends it to my father, who also has one of these little boxes."

KEY IDEA

Pessimists let their sight limit their reality. Optimists let their vision become their reality. That's why optimism is always more realistic than pessimism.

The time traveler decides to humor me. "So what are you and your father talking about?"

"He's flying out here tomorrow to see me, and I need to know when to pick him up."

With this answer, the time traveler thinks I am absolutely nuts. Not only am I bouncing my voice off of floating objects in outer space, my father is flying all the way across the country in a day. He says, "If your father is flying here tomorrow, you had better plan to scrape him up rather than pick him up." Then he walks away shaking his head.

Any realistic person living in the nineteenth century would know that neither of these could be done. People don't fly and voices don't bounce across the country. Yet today, that's our reality.

Cell phones, satellite communication, and jet travel aren't things that just became possible in the last hundred years. Since the dawn of mankind, they have always been possible. They just weren't invented until recently. What made them possible are the laws of physics, and the laws of physics have always been the same. We didn't recently invent them. We just learned how to harness them. They were harnessed by some very optimistic people who kept working despite the cries from countless pessimists to stop.

KEY IDEA

The reality we have today was created by optimistic people who ignored the cries of the pessimists saying, "It can't be done."

When I think of all the really strange things that are commonplace today, I am afraid to label anything impossible. In fact, when students use the word impossible, I hand them my office dictionary. "Look up the word 'impossible.'" They look and look but they can't find it. A long time ago, I took a pair of scissors and cut the word impossible out of my dictionary. Now there is a hole where the word "impossible" used to be. I tell them that I don't believe in impossible.

DR. BIG DUMB JOCK

The limits of what we see as possible are constantly changing because of changing technology. In a similar way, the limits of what you and I can do should also be changing. We have near limitless potential to accomplish anything we put our minds to because we have near limitless possibility to change.

If you want to know how much people can change in a short time, ask anyone who knew me in high school. Now I'm called Professor Muncy. Now I'm Dr. Muncy. Back then, I was known as the Big Dumb Jock. Studying wasn't a high priority on my list. Actually, it never made my list at all. I saw school as the thing you did while waiting for basketball practice. The only thought I ever gave to grades was how I could explain mine to the coach.

After graduating from high school and piddling around at a junior college for a little while, I tried out for the basketball team of a small college nearby. I earned a full scholarship. I knew I could eventually work my way onto the starting squad, but then what? Not many pro scouts were showing up at Wayland Baptist University in search of talent. Given my level of commitment to basketball, I knew I didn't have much future in the game. So, just as quickly as I walked onto the team, I walked off.

I drifted onto the campus of the big state university nearby. There,

I decided to try something I had never done before. I decided to try studying. I set the goal of graduating with honors. I signed up for an overload my first semester and went after it.

I was amazed. That studying thing actually worked. I made very good grades and continued to do so until I graduated on time with honors. I didn't see any reason to quit there. I wasn't burned out on studying. After all, I hadn't been doing it for very long and I was just starting to get the hang of it. I went on to graduate school, and within a few years, I earned my Ph.D.

By my ten-year high school reunion, I was teaching at the University of Oklahoma. I couldn't wait to show up and hear all my old classmates tell me how proud they were of me.

The first person I wanted to look up was Mark Redus. He was Mr. Everything in high school. He was all-district running back two years in a row. Out of almost six hundred students, he graduated in the top twenty. He was voted the most popular guy in the whole school. Our high school yearbook looked like his personal photo album. He had it all. Mark and I had been friends. In fact, I was a groomsman in his wedding. However, we lost touch, so he didn't know what I had accomplished.

As soon as I saw him at the reunion, I went right over to him. I asked him what he was doing, and he told me he was in graduate school. He asked me what I was doing. I told him I was a professor at the University of Oklahoma. I waited for the smile. I waited for the words of affirmation. I waited for "I knew you could do it." Instead, I got a look as if to say, "You obviously didn't understand my question."

I told him that I had earned my Ph.D. and that I was now teaching at OU. Silence. It seemed like an hour, but I am sure it was only a few seconds. He was obviously trying to reconcile totally incongruent pieces of information. I could almost see him thinking: "Muncy, lousy student; now Muncy, Ph.D., Professor …. What's wrong with this picture?" I will never forget the first words out of his mouth. "You are the absolute last person I would have ever expected to earn a Ph.D." Just in case I missed it, he said it again. "You are the absolute last person I would have ever expected to earn a Ph.D." He walked away looking as though he needed a little time to figure this one out.

Not one, single person said, "I knew you could do it." Several people asked, "So what are you really doing?" I am still not sure many people at the reunion believed that the class Big Dumb Jock was now Dr. Big-But-Not-Dumb-After-All Jock.

Actually, the Jim Muncy they knew did not earn his Ph.D. He couldn't have done it. It took a substantially improved version of Jim Muncy. Sure, the kid they knew in high school wasn't academic material. Fortunately for me, I wasn't stuck with that kid. When I decided I wanted more in life, all I had to do was change.

HE WHO MUST, CAN

There is a Yiddish proverb that says, "He who must, can." I tell my students that any one of them could make straight A's. When I do, out comes the negative, pessimistic thinking. "You don't know what I face. I have Professor Jerk this semester. He never gives A's. I am working forty hours per week. You can't make straight A's working forty hours …." I've heard plenty of reasons why they won't try, but I've never heard one single reason why they could not succeed.

To prove my point, I give them the following scenario. Imagine that the person you love most in this world is gravely ill. If she doesn't get a very expensive operation, she will die. I will pay for the operation if and only if you make all A's this semester. Then I ask, "Under those circumstances, which one of you could not make straight A's this or any semester?"

I have never had a student say, "No, I could not." I have taught around ten thousand students in my career. Without one single exception, the goal of making straight A's would have been realistic for every single one of them.

That's the way it is in life. If we must do something, we can do it. That means if we don't do something, it isn't because we can't. It is because we choose not to.

Does that mean we can do anything? Absolutely not. There are some things I know I could never ever do. I have a six-foot-five-inch body on a very large frame. Even when testing out at an extra-lean body weight, I am still over two

KEY IDEA

Regardless of what we can't do, there are some pretty incredible things we can do.

hundred fifty pounds. If the life of my wife Lisa was on the line, and I had to ride the winning racehorse at the Kentucky Derby to save her, we would just have to start making funeral arrangements. I couldn't do it no matter how hard I tried.

We can't do everything, but the number of things we can do greatly outnumbers the number of things we can't do. I may never be a champion racehorse jockey. Still, I can live a pretty good life and accomplish some pretty incredible things even if I never see a racehorse.

It is foolish to let our limitations make us pessimistic. Think of Helen Keller. I have never met a person who was as limited as she. Without sight or hearing, she had plenty of reasons to be pessimistic. She never let her limitations slow her down. In her life, presidents were proud to be counted among her friends. She was decorated by royalty. There was a lot that she couldn't do, but she always remained optimistic, knowing that she could do something. She once said:

> "I am only one, but still I am one. I cannot do everything, but still I can do something; and because I cannot do everything, I will not refuse to do the something that I can do."

Like Helen Keller, we should never let our limitations detract from the incredible things we can do. Regardless of what we can't do, there are some pretty incredible things we can do.

OPTIMISM CREATES CONFIDENCE, NOT ARROGANCE

KEY IDEA

Confidence is knowing that we will succeed if we do the right things and knowing that we are capable of doing the right things.

Optimism is a type of confidence. Confidence is critical for our success. Unfortunately, some people have confused confidence with arrogance. The difference is huge.

Let's say I wanted to take a cruise ship across the ocean. I would want the captain and crew to be confident. What would I think if I showed up to board the ship and all the crew members were wearing life jackets? I wouldn't feel too good if I heard the first mate making a speech that started with "I know many of you don't think this old ship can make it across one more time, but let's cross our fingers and hope for the best. If anything goes wrong, meet me at the life boats ...." I would be real concerned if I glanced over to the life boats and the captain had moved his bunk inside one of them just in case.

Would I board that ship? Absolutely not. I am not jumping on board any ship unless the crew is absolutely 100% confident they can get me safely to my destination—and back!

On the other hand, I am not boarding a ship if I think the captain and crew are arrogant either. It wasn't an iceberg that sank the *Titanic*. It was arrogance. Hundreds of ships crossed that very same ice field where the *Titanic* sank. The crews of these other ships were confident they could navigate around the icebergs, and they took the precautions necessary to avoid disaster. They slowed down and treated the area with respect. They knew one wrong move could sink their ship.

Not the crew of the *Titanic*. They must have heard one too many times that even God couldn't sink the *Titanic*. They ignored the warnings from other ships in the vicinity. They steamed on ahead through the night. While the confident crews of other ships were doing the things necessary to avoid the ice, the arrogant crew of the *Titanic* believed they would make it across no matter what they did. Navigating icebergs is not a big deal. Ships' crews confidently do it all the time. It was when the crew of *Titanic* moved from being confident to being arrogant that their ship sank.

Confidence says I can do it if I do the right things, and I am capable of doing the right things. Arrogance believes that success is ensured because of who I am and nothing can stop me—even my failure to do the things success requires. Arrogance doesn't stem from optimism. It stems from stupidity, and a failure to understand the very nature of success. Arrogance is a huge liability. Genuine optimism breeds genuine confidence, and that is always an asset.

CONFIDENT IN WHAT?

There are three main types of confidence. The greatest confidence is the belief in something greater than one's self. In many people's lives, this confidence takes the form of a spiritual faith. To others, it's a belief in a cause or greater

> **KEY IDEA**
>
> *The two great potentials in life are the potential to grow and the potential to discover.*

purpose. As long as this belief isn't misguided, then this faith or belief can be an incredible force that can move people to do amazing things. People like Susan B. Anthony, Martin Luther King, Mother Teresa, and Albert Schweitzer, as well as many others, literally changed the world when they went forth with a confidence that was based on something much bigger than themselves.

A second type of confidence is self-confidence. Here, you have confidence that you can do something because you have done so in the past. In some realms, I am quite confident. In others, I am not. If I were having surgery, I would want every member of the medical team to have a confidence that comes from experience. I wouldn't want the surgeon to get inside my chest and say, "What's that thing moving around in there? Oh, it's the heart. What is it in there for?" With self-confidence, we can continue doing well the things we already do well.

However, self-confidence won't get us to take on newer and bigger challenges. That requires optimism. Optimism is the third type of confidence. **Optimism is a confidence in our potential**. Specifically, it is a belief in the incredible potential within each of us to do great things. A pessimist does not hold such a belief. Just as an atheist is defined as a person who does not believe in God, a pessimist can be defined as a person who does not believe in potential.

We become optimistic when we discover the two great potentials of life. These are the potential to grow and the potential to discover. Let's look at each.

THE POTENTIAL TO GROW

KEY IDEA

To reach our potential, growth isn't optional. It is required.

If I set my sights in life based on **who I am**, then what I now have is all I can ever have. When I set goals based on **who I can become**, my potential becomes astounding. We must not look at who we are as the measure of what we can do. We must look at who we can become.

Have you ever been to the circus and seen the elephant acts? Out comes a huge elephant being led by a little guy holding onto a thin rope. He takes this little bitty stake, pounds it into the ground, and then ties the elephant to it. This huge hunk of muscle is tied down by a rope that he could snap if he sneezed and a stake that would pop out of the ground with the slightest of tugs. Still, the elephant will never escape. He can't escape. He is tied down by something much more powerful than the rope and the stake. He is tied down by the BELIEF that he is tied down by the rope and the stake.

Here is what happened. The elephant was captured as a baby. The hunters took a huge rope and tied one end to the little elephant and the other end to a giant tree. For days upon days, the baby elephant tugged and tugged trying to escape. Finally, the little elephant gave up. It learned it was helpless, and it never again tried to escape.

The elephant grew but he didn't understand growth. The elephant changed, but he didn't understand change. The rope grew smaller, and the huge tree became a tiny stake, but the elephant never noticed the difference. The elephant stayed trapped in the reality of the baby elephant tied to the big tree—a prisoner of a reality that no longer existed.

We must not make this elephant-sized mistake. We must not let ourselves be trapped in a reality that disappeared many years ago. If we commit ourselves to growing bigger and stronger, the reality that we are prisoners of today will quickly disappear. We may be small now, and we may be tied to something huge. The odds may be against us. That isn't the way it always has to be. We can outgrow our challenges.

Prior to the day Sir Edmund Hillary successfully climbed Mount Everest, many tried and failed. After one failed expedition in which a few climbers perished, the survivors threw a banquet to honor those lost. Across the front wall of the banquet hall was a huge picture of Mount Everest. When the speaker stood up, he did not address the audience. He turned and addressed the picture. Here is what he said.

"Everest, you have defeated us once. Everest, you have defeated us twice. Everest, you have defeated us three times. But Everest, one day we will defeat you because you can't get any bigger but we can."

Eventually, Everest was defeated because we did get bigger. No matter how big the mountain is that we are trying to climb, it is not getting bigger. Hopefully, we are.

KEYS TO GROWTH

Our potential to achieve is almost limitless. However, to achieve our potential, growth is not optional. It is required. That's why we must look at ways to grow. There are four things we can do to make sure we are growing so that we can achieve more and more of our potential every day.

Put Ourselves into 'Must Grow' Situations

All of us face situations where we see something we would like to do in our lives, but we think we don't have the ability to do it. That is when we have one of two choices we could make. We can either walk away from what we want, or we can make the decision to become the person who can do it. Certainly the most comfortable thing to do is to simply walk away and not even try. We must resist that temptation with all we have. Here's why.

If we refuse to try new things, we pass up a great opportunity to grow. Instead of walking away from such situations, we should embrace them. We should want to put ourselves into must-grow situations. Growth is difficult, and we just won't do the work if there isn't a prize for doing it. It is those times when something catches our eye and we need to grow to have success that we can have both the environment in which to grow and the motivation to do so. In the end, we will have both the prize and the growth. The next time we are faced with the same desire, we won't even be tempted to walk away.

We shouldn't set goals that we can achieve with who we are. There's no growth there. We should set goals based on the growth that must occur for us to reach them. Then, when we have reached the goal, we won't just have a victory. We will also have a new and improved version of ourselves. A great entertainer once said, "I do things I can't do. That's how I get to where I can do them."

Make Every Opportunity a Learning Experience

A person was interviewing for a sales job. His resume showed that he had been in sales for twenty years. The manager interviewing him asked the tough question. Pointing to his experience, the interviewer asked, "Does this mean you have twenty years of sales experience or that you have one year of sales experience twenty times?" Good question.

Some say "Practice makes perfect." Not so. Practice makes permanent. If you do the wrong thing over and over, you aren't getting perfect. You are getting stuck in a bad habit.

Several summers ago, I found myself with very little to do. I was teaching at Texas Tech at the time, but I had accepted a position at

Clemson University half-way across the country. The new job started in the fall. I had finished up all my research projects, and it made no sense to start any new ones until I got to Clemson. So that summer became my summer of golf.

At the start of the summer, my brother came to visit me from California. We went out to a local course to see what we could do. Neither of us did very well, but I won the round. That gave me the mistaken impression that, with just a little practice, I could become good at the game. So I spent that whole summer playing golf every day. Sometimes I would play eighteen holes and start over and play another eighteen.

KEY IDEA

Progressive practice makes perfect.

At the end of the summer, I went to visit my brother. He had not picked up a club since our last game, and I had spent my whole summer practicing. We played a round of golf and he beat me. My summer of practice didn't make me any better. It just set in stone all the things I was doing wrong.

I have not played golf in years, and I will not play golf until I take the time to learn it the right way. If I don't have time to take lessons from a knowledgeable golf pro, I am not playing the game. Hopefully by then I will have recovered from all my practice and will be back at zero. Practice doesn't make perfect. Practice makes permanent.

Rick Pitino has modified that old proverb. He says perfect practice makes perfect. I'm not sure I agree with that, either. If my practice is already perfect, then I am not making perfection. I am maintaining it. When I eventually do venture onto the golf course, I feel certain that even the best pro on the planet won't be able to launch me into the realm of perfect practice. Perfect practice maintains perfection.

Let me propose a better saying: Progressive practice makes perfect. I should never keep doing the same thing over and over the same way unless I have already perfected it. My goal is to take every effort and analyze it by asking two questions. I should ask myself "What did I do right?" No matter how bad my performance was, I did something right. The other question is "What should I do differently?"

Notice I didn't say "What did I do wrong?" If we think about what we did wrong, we will repeat it. It is as if we are telling our mind to practice the wrong thing. I have had several students who were lifeguards. They tell me that if they see a child running and they yell "Don't run," the kid just keeps on running. On the other hand, if they yell "Walk," the child will walk. In the same way, we shouldn't be telling ourselves what we don't want to do. We should be thinking about how to do it right.

KEY IDEA

As kids, growth is a natural part of life. When we hit about twenty years old, growth starts to take effort.

Make Growth Part of Our Daily Routine

Growth is a natural part of life until we are about twenty years old. After that, it takes a conscious effort to keep growing. If we don't make the conscious effort, we quit growing.

One of my favorite church services has always been the night the children's choirs sing. The youngest preschool choir always steals the show. They are so cute. They don't really sing. Some scream and some whisper. They all wiggle. Some forget the music and spend their whole time looking for Mommy. There is always one little girl who stands there lifting her dress up over her head. It is cute to see these kids standing there doing something that doesn't even approximate singing. The performance is great because it is preschoolers being preschoolers.

I don't think it would be quite so cute if the adult choir came in on Sunday morning and did what these little children do. Instead of singing, some were yelling, some were whispering, and a few were looking for their mommies. How funny would it be if over weight and middle-aged Ms. Smith started lifting her dress up over her head? Not funny at all. The choir director would probably get fired.

We expect kids to act like kids. We also expect there to be a maturing process as they get older. We expect the kindergarten choir to be a little more mature than the toddlers. We expect the high school choir to have more musical ability than the junior high choir.

We would think that something was terribly wrong if someone was acting exactly the same at fifteen as he did at five. But we don't seem to be nearly as concerned about the thirty-five-year-old that has not grown much since he was twenty-five. All around us there are people who have gone from ages thirty to fifty with no noticeable growth in their lives. The tragedy is that people who refuse to grow are not very introspective, so they don't see the tragedy in their own lives.

Here's the problem. As kids, growth is a natural part of life. Children don't have to do anything to mature. That comes with being a child. As adults, this natural maturing process ceases. Somewhere around twenty, growth starts to take effort. Unless we do something specific to make sure we are growing, it stops.

We must make sure that this growth continues by making it part of our daily routine. Eating is part of my daily routine. So is taking a shower. It's taken some effort, but I have also made exercise something I do every day. We have all these routine things we do to make sure our bodies are taken care of. We need some routine to make sure our brains are also in good shape.

We should make it a habit of reading twenty minutes to an hour every day from material that will improve our mind power. We shouldn't waste all the time we spend in the car listening to the radio. Buy some personal development audio series and pop them into the stereo instead. With a few simple changes, we can start taking care of our minds like we take care of our bodies.

Get Around People Who Challenge Us

The fourth key to growth is to get around people who are where we want to be. If I wanted to, I could always find a basketball game where I could be the star. I may have to go to the elementary school to find it, but I can always find someone, somewhere who can make me look good.

However, slam dunking over third graders is not going to do much to improve my game. If I want to get better, I look to play with people who are better than I. When I play against them, I don't look nearly as impressive, but I get better. The better the people I am around, the better I become. This is true in all areas of our lives. Again, we come back to the incredible impact the people around us have on who we become.

Those are the keys to growth. We can achieve incredible things if we are learning and doing the right things around the right people. It is up to us to make these things happen. When we do, we release one of the two great potentials in life—the potential to grow.

THE POTENTIAL TO DISCOVER

A second great potential that most people fail to nurture is the potential to discover solutions to our problems. David Schwartz tells a story that is an indictment of my profession. One time, there was a kid who wanted to grow up and own his own business. When he finished high school, he went off to the university to study business administration. While he was there, he learned all the things you need to start a business.

He learned that you couldn't start a business unless you were adequately capitalized. He learned that you couldn't start a business unless you had a competitive advantage. He learned that you couldn't start a business unless you had established distributor relations. He didn't have any of the things you need to start a business, and so when he graduated, he went to work for someone else.

A few years later, he ran into a friend from high school. This friend was a successful business owner. He didn't go to college and learn all the things you need to start a business. He just went ahead and started his business. It didn't take him long to realize he needed money, so he figured out a way to get the money he needed. When he found out he needed people to sell his products, he found them. He quickly learned that he couldn't survive if he was like everyone else, so he changed. He didn't wait until he had all the problems solved before he opened his doors. He solved the problems as they came along. If we wait until we have all the things we need to start a business, we will never start a business.

Seldom do we discover things we need before we need them. It is our needs that lead to discoveries. A number of years ago, when I had just married, a new department store came to town. Several of our friends who happened to have small children at the time told us about how great it was, so Lisa and I went to check it out. It was a total disappointment. We didn't see anything in the store that appealed to us. We vowed to never go back.

A few years later, we had small children of our own. We wandered into that same store, and were surprised to discover it was the best store we had ever seen. Everything in it was designed just for us. We could have spent a whole year's paychecks there in one visit.

Later, I read about this company's strategy. It was targeting families with children, and all their products were selected with that group in mind. Without children, I would see these products and walk right by them. They didn't address any of the needs I had at the time. A few years later, when we had children, I walked through the very same store and saw all kinds of things I needed. The store hadn't changed. My needs changed.

KEY IDEA

Solutions come after problems, not before.

Our attention is need driven. At any moment, we are only attuned to whatever it is that we need at that moment. We ignore things we don't need right now. On the other hand, if we need something, we will spot it in an instant if it is anywhere to be found.

Even if we lack everything we need to accomplish something, we can still be optimistic. Once we decide on a goal and start moving in the direction of that goal, we will be amazed at all the things we discover along the way that are just what we need to achieve it. However, this process of discovery can't begin until we set the goal.

Solutions come after the problem, not before. Even if we see solutions right in front of our face, they hold no significance to us until we face the problem. We will walk right by them. But once we are ready for the solution, we see it. As the ancient saying goes, "When the student is ready, the teacher will appear."

One time, I was the banquet speaker for a large group of salespeople. The person who asked me to speak said morale was down and she wanted me to give a talk that would lift everyone's spirits. It didn't take me long to figure out where the morale problem was.

My talk followed a combined presentation by the regional vice president and the regional director of sales. They gave a "sky is falling" speech. The company made some changes that would make it harder to sell its product. The competition was also increasing in one of their major markets. By the time these two were through talking, my audience was asking the servers to bring out the hemlock.

I had something I wanted to say to the depressing duo, but I didn't want to address them directly. In the middle of my speech I sent a message to them. I didn't look at them when I gave it, but here's what I said.

"Remove all the challenges and eliminate all the problems from your job, and anyone could do it. In your job, you will face significant

KEY IDEA

Big opportunities come with big problems. Big rewards don't come from solving small problems.

challenges. You will need to solve some big problems. Be glad you do because if it weren't for these problems, you would be expendable. Anyone could do your job. Your company doesn't need someone with your qualifications to do the detailed part of your job. They need someone with your qualifications to solve the big problems. Take the problems away, and you lose half your income."

Opportunities will always come our way. When they do, they will be mixed with problems. Thomas Edison said that the reason many people don't recognize opportunity is that it shows up in overalls looking a lot like work. If you're looking for opportunities without problems, you won't find them. The bigger the opportunity, the bigger the problems; the bigger the problems, the bigger the opportunity.

We have two ways to respond when opportunities show up mixed with problems. We can see the problems and walk away because we don't immediately know how to solve them. We may go looking for smaller problems. If we want smaller problems, we can find them. They will be attached to smaller opportunities. We will find small opportunities with small problems and have small successes.

If we want big successes, we will take a different approach. We will accept big challenges. When we do, we will unleash the creative power of our mind to solve the big problems that come with big opportunities. Solutions to the problems we see will show up after we have accepted the challenge and gone to work on it. We can't wait for all the lights to be green before we get in our car for a trip.

GET YOUR HOPES UP

Through creativity and growth we can achieve incredible things. That is why any realistic person is optimistic. Have you ever heard someone say, "I just don't want you to get your hopes up," as if there is something wrong with us getting our hopes up? That is exactly what we must do. We must get our hopes up. It is hope that motivates us. It is our hopes that push us on to great things.

Remember Apollo 13. It was almost to the moon when their space ship went boom. "Houston, we have a problem." Boy, did they have a problem. When Houston realized what that problem was, what did they say? "Guys, we'll do our best to bring you back to Earth, but don't get your hopes up." No, they said, "We will bring you home safely!"

It was a long shot. The space ship was severely damaged. They didn't have the power they needed. The oxygen supply was in danger of being cut off. Still, the command center proceeded with absolute confidence that they would find a way to get astronauts Lovell, Swigert, and Haise back to Earth alive. It took every brain cell NASA had to figure out solutions to the problems they faced, but it was hope that kept them working day and night. In the end, hope won out and the crew was saved.

This life has three great things to offer: faith, hope, and love. That's it. If we lose any one of them, then we have lost a big chunk of what makes life worth living. Never say, "I don't want you to get your hopes up." That's taking away one of the greatest things in life.

Things don't always work out like we want them to. That's why hope always brings with it the potential for pain. We can kill the hope to kill the pain, but in that case the solution is worse than the problem. That's like going bird hunting with a cannon. Sure, you may kill a few birds, but you'll never find their remains.

Don't avoid disappointment by eliminating hope. Instead, we need to keep the hope and learn to handle disappointments. Once we develop the ability to handle our disappointments, we won't be afraid to be optimistic. At that point, we will have moved a long way toward thinking the way successful people think.

KEY 3

There are reasons and results. And reasons don't count.
—Burke Hedges, speaker and trainer

RESPONSIBILITY: THINK RESULTS, NOT REASONS

A boy had spent several months following his grandfather around the golf course. He got a set of toy clubs for his birthday. With great excitement, he headed off to the back yard to show everyone how well he had learned to play golf from his grandfather. With his whole family watching, Junior proudly picked the first club out of the bag. But rather than hitting a ball with it, he threw it into a tree and started cursing at it.

Obviously this boy had learned something from his grandfather. He didn't learn how to play golf. He had learned to play the blame game. When the grandfather missed the shot, he blamed the club. Perhaps that's why the club kept making the same mistake over and over.

Gilbert Arland made an interesting observation. He said, "When an archer misses the mark, he turns and looks for the fault within himself. Failure to hit the bull's-eye is never the fault of the target. To improve your aim, improve yourself." That's a key to success.

Every failure to achieve results has its reasons. Unfortunately, reasons are no substitute for results. As long as we are making excuses for poor performance, that's all we will ever have—excuses and poor performance. To achieve high levels of success, we must train our minds to think results, not reasons.

AVOID LAZY THINKING

One of my students' favorite books to read is *Rich Dad, Poor Dad* by Robert Kiyosaki. Kiyosaki's real father, whom he calls his poor dad, was well educated but struggled financially all of his life. Kiyosaki called his best friend's father his rich dad. The rich dad didn't have the education of the poor dad, yet he was able to amass a fortune. While

KEY IDEA

"I can't" usually means "I don't want to try."

he was growing up, Kiyosaki noticed that his rich dad and his poor dad were always giving him different advice. Kiyosaki explains how people who are rich think differently than those who are poor or middle class. This book clearly shows that how you think determines where you end up in life.

One day when Kiyosaki was a child, he went to his poor dad and asked if he could have a bicycle. His father said no. When Kiyosaki asked why, his father said they couldn't afford one. Later, his rich dad saw that something was wrong and asked him what was the matter. "I want a bicycle, but we can't afford one."

"Don't ever say that," Kiyosaki's rich dad responded. "Never say 'I can't afford something.' That's lazy thinking. Ask 'How can I afford it?'" Then Kiyosaki's rich dad went on to explain what he meant.

By saying I can't afford something, I excuse myself from having to do the hard work of thinking. When we want something, there is almost always an ethical and legal way to get it. However, the way to get it might not be readily apparent. It may require significant mental effort to figure it out. It may require reading and studying. It may require talking to people and searching out answers. It may require analyzing and evaluating things in ways that might stretch your thinking.

"But if we say, 'I can't afford it,' we don't have to put out all this effort. If, on the other hand, we ask how we can afford it, we are forcing ourselves to think. To say, 'I can't afford it' before we have even gone to work looking for a way to afford it is mental laziness. 'I can't' really means 'I don't want to try.'"

GOODBYE TO OUR COMFORTABLE EXCUSES

Successful thinking is optimistic thinking. However, optimistic thinking is not always comfortable thinking. Indeed, we do gain an incredible sense of empowerment when we realize that we can do almost anything we set our minds to do. However, we lose all the excuses that have given us such great comfort throughout the years. "I can't" is not longer a viable excuse. If I don't do something, it is because I have chosen not to do it. I can no longer play the helpless damsel in distress or powerless victim. I have what I have because of the choices I have made, and I am responsible for those choices.

One time, I was teaching a class and the topic for the day was responsibility. I told my students that they can do almost anything they wanted to do. I said that we shouldn't make excuses when the real reason for our failure is that we didn't try. Little did I know how quickly my words would come back and smack me in the face.

After class, a student walked up to me. About a month earlier, she had given me one of her past exams and asked me to look at something she thought I had misgraded. She wanted to know if I had done so. "I'm sorry," I said. "I haven't had time to look it over."

She looked at me as if I was the biggest hypocrite on the planet. I had just spent an hour telling students that we must take responsibility for our own actions. I had told them that we can do pretty much anything we want to do. I had explained that "I can't" means "I choose not to." Now, here I was telling her I didn't have five minutes in a whole month to look over her exam.

In the last month, I had time to look over my emails. In the last month, I had found time to eat three meals a day. Whenever I heard a good joke over the last months, I found time to wander past offices looking for colleagues to tell the joke to. I had found time to play basketball in the last month. Sure, I live a busy life, but in the previous month, I had found time to do all the things I really wanted to do. I just hadn't found time to do all the things I should have done.

As soon as I realized what I was doing, I looked her straight in the eye and said, "I am sorry. I should have made the time to look it over and I didn't. I did not live up to my responsibility, and for that I sincerely apologize. I will have it back to you next class period." That day, I found the time to look over her exam.

CLOSED DOORS DON'T KEEP US OUT

How many times have we heard someone use the expression "The door was closed" when explaining why they didn't do something. Locked doors don't keep us out of buildings if we really want to go

KEY IDEA

When we lack passion, we look for open doors. When we are totally set on a goal, brick walls can't hold us back.

inside. Sure, I've walked up to a door, turned the handle to discover it was locked, and walked away. It wasn't the door that stopped me. It was my decision that whatever was inside wasn't worth what it would cost me to get inside.

What if the building were on fire and my children were on the other side of that door. Would I walk up to the door, jiggle the handle to find it was locked and walk away? Absolutely not! Whatever it took, I would get through that door. When we aren't passionate about what we are doing, we look for open doors. When we are totally set on a particular goal, brick walls can't hold us back. We shouldn't blame the locking of doors when the real problem is our lacking of desire.

OBSTACLES VERSUS ROADBLOCKS

Obviously, things can happen which can hold us back. As I said in the previous chapter, we cannot do everything. But we can do almost anything. We must learn to tell the difference between obstacles and roadblocks.

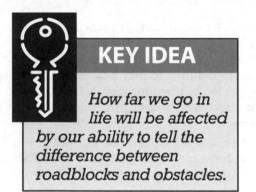

KEY IDEA

How far we go in life will be affected by our ability to tell the difference between roadblocks and obstacles.

If I take a trip, I can anticipate that there will be obstacles along the way. There will be pot-holes and debris in the road. I may encounter road construction or stalled cars. These are to be expected. When I do happen upon an obstacle, I simply go around it. I don't cancel the family vacation and return home the first time I have to go around a chunk of blown truck tire on the interstate. I figure the easiest way around it and I keep going.

There are times, however, when we encounter roadblocks. Not far from my house, a bridge was washed out, so the county put up a roadblock. When I first came upon that roadblock, I didn't blindly zip around it and go driving off the bridge. Whereas obstacles don't stop us, roadblocks do.

Even when we are stopped by a roadblock, we don't just sit there and stare at it forever. We might need to re-route our trip. Depending on the reason for the roadblock, we may even need to postpone or cancel our trip. But we don't stop traveling because at one time in our life we encountered a roadblock.

In life, obstacles abound. We can't plan our trip around them. If we let them turn us back, we will never get anywhere. We must simply head on through life expecting obstacles, and when we encounter them, deal with them in the most expedient way possible.

In life, there are much fewer roadblocks. When we encounter a roadblock, we stop what we are doing and regroup. We look to see if there is another way to get where we want to go. There usually is, but if there is not, we re-evaluate our destination.

When I was in graduate school, I was at a party. There was a very attractive and interesting woman there named Gerry. By the end of the evening, I had stars in my eyes. When I got back to my apartment, I told my roommate I wanted to ask her out on a date. He gave me a strange look. He told me Gerry was married. Now, I had not encountered an obstacle. This was a roadblock. The stars in my eyes quickly faded and Gerry was no longer on my list of people I might ask out on a date.

Just because I encountered one roadblock, that didn't mean that I never went on a date for the rest of my life. About a year later, I met someone else who I really liked. Unfortunately, I had already accepted a job six hours away. We had such a great time together, I decided to go ahead and date her anyway. I have to admit that the distance between us was a pain. Still, it was an obstacle, not a roadblock. We dealt with it, and I am glad that we did because we eventually got married, and I have enjoyed many great years with my wife, Lisa.

How far we go in life will be determined by our ability to tell the difference between an obstacle and a roadblock. If we are in the habit of zipping past roadblocks, we will drive off a lot of bridges. On the other hand, if we stop at every obstacle along the way, we will never go very far. Let's explore how we should make this call.

ETHICAL ROADBLOCKS

When it comes to moral issues, we should be quick to see something as a roadblock. Anything that is close to immoral or unethical should be seen as a roadblock.

There was a wealthy man who lived atop a high mountain. To get to and from his house, he had to travel a winding road with high and steep cliffs right at the edge. He needed a new chauffeur and was interviewing

KEY IDEA

On ethical issues, we should be quick to see things as roadblocks. On all other issues, we should do just the opposite.

candidates and had narrowed the list down to three people. He had one question he wanted to ask them, and their answer would decide which one he would hire.

He asked the first candidate how close he could get to the edge of the road without driving off the cliff. Candidate One replied that he could consistently get within two feet and never swerve off the edge.

He asked the second candidate the same question. This candidate said he could always drive within one foot of the side and never crash.

Then he asked the third candidate how close he could drive to the edge. "I'm not sure," he answered, "but I will tell you this. I am staying as far away from the edge as I can." Candidate Three got the job.

That is how we should set the standard on ethical issues. We shouldn't see how close we can get to the line. Our goal should be to stay as far away from the edge as we can.

How High of a Standard?

When it comes to issues that aren't ethical or moral, our standard should do just the opposite. We should try to see everything as an obstacle and not as a roadblock.

One time, I was teaching a series of lessons about someone who had achieved a level of success that was unmatched by anyone I have ever known or even heard of. The interesting thing about this person is that he never seemed to accept excuses from anyone. Though he was a very loving person, he seemed to love people too much to allow them to make excuses. I concluded that one of the key components of this person's character was his ability to love people totally while never accepting excuses from them. I call this the "blame buster" lesson.

On my way out the door one morning, I was sharing my blame-buster lesson with my wife and four children. When I opened the front door, all I could see was garbage strewn all over our front yard. This happens every time one of us doesn't put the trash in the trashcan, which is located inside a fenced area around the side of the house. If the garbage bag is tossed over the fence and lands outside the garbage can, some neighborhood dog tears into the bag, and decorates our front yard with trash.

"Who didn't put the trash where it goes?" I asked, looking at our four children. I saw three kids pointing fingers and one kid wishing he were somewhere else. "When we get home, you will have to clean up this mess," I said to him. "Also, you miss out on our next dessert." That's our standard penalty for not putting the trash inside the garbage can.

My child responded, "But it was real dark last night. You know I hate the dark. It was raining and cold. I didn't want to get all wet, and I hate to get cold. I didn't think a dog would get to it."

"You've got to do better than that," I said. "Those excuses aren't nearly as good as some of the unacceptable ones in my blame-buster lesson." Then, I turned to address all four of our kids. "As a matter of a fact, we have this new rule around the house. If your excuse isn't at least as good as the blame-buster ones, they don't qualify."

That was when we established a new standard for the excuses we would accept around our household. It didn't take me long to realize that I hadn't thought things through before I set the standards. The problem wasn't with the kids. They adjusted quite well. The problem was that the kids started expecting me to live by the same standard. Some of the excuses I had been giving around the house suddenly started to seem pretty lame. After the kids called me on a few lame excuses, I started questioning why I set such a high standard.

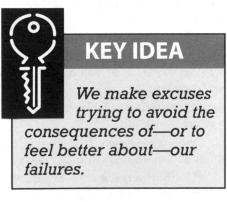

KEY IDEA

We make excuses trying to avoid the consequences of—or to feel better about—our failures.

However, in the end, I'm glad I did. By instituting the blame-buster lesson, I've discovered that living life by such a high standard yields incredible results. We may never totally reach the standard, but it is certainly worth shooting for. The higher the standard we set for roadblocks, the less tolerance we have for excuses, and the further we will go in life. Why? Because every time we make an excuse, we stop making progress. When we lower our standards for excuses, we invariably lower our standards for achievement.

When it comes right down to it, there are really only two reasons why we make excuses. We make excuses trying to avoid the consequences or to feel better about our failures. Neither of these is good, and let's see why.

LIFE DOESN'T ALLOW EXEMPTIONS

R.C. was a professor who had his students turn in five assignments one semester. In the syllabus he handed out the first day of class, he listed the due dates for each of the papers. He also said that no papers would be accepted late. Any paper turned in late would get a zero. The consequences were set.

The first assignment came due and two students came to R.C. with great fear and trembling. They had incredible excuses as to why they didn't have their papers done. No problem, he said, you can just turn them in next week.

The next assignment came due and a few more students came to him with some fear but no trembling. They all had good excuses, and he let them turn in their assignments late. Then the third and fourth assignments came along. He experienced more late papers, no fear, and a bunch of lousy excuses.

Then came the day he was to collect the last assignment. He called for the papers. "No problem," the students responded with no concern whatsoever in their voices. "This was a tough week. We'll get them to you next week."

"Where is your paper, John?" R.C. asked. "You don't have it. That is a zero."

John went nuts. "That's not fair. I'll get it to you next week. I had to study for an exam in another class."

"John, you get a zero. Susan, where is your paper? No paper, that's a zero. Tom … zero. Ashley … zero." On and on he went. Every student who didn't turn in their papers on time got a zero for the assignment, and most of them had to repeat the course.

R.C. was not being unfair for making his students turn in their assignment on time. They knew from the first day of class when he would collect their papers. Three months is an adequate time for any student under any circumstances to have a paper ready to turn in. Where R.C. went wrong was that he had built up the expectation in the students' minds that they could get away with excuses. When he did, the students started working harder on their excuses than they did on their papers.

People like me often accept a lot more excuses than we should. Do you know why we do so? It's not because we are kind. Letting people get into the habit of making excuses is an extremely unkind thing to do. We accept excuses because it is the easiest thing for us to do.

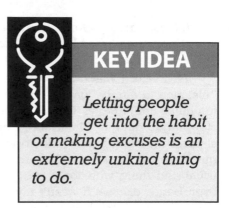

KEY IDEA

Letting people get into the habit of making excuses is an extremely unkind thing to do.

As a professor, it costs me so little to accept an excuse. I recently had a student who overslept and missed an exam. What did I do? I let him make it up. Did I do so because I thought it was in the best interest of the student? Absolutely not. I did so because it was in my best interest. It was easier to just give him a makeup exam during my office hours than it was to hassle with telling him that he got a zero. I didn't have to be the jerk.

He thought I was a nice guy. In reality, I was being lazy, and I was teaching him a terrible lesson. My laziness was teaching him that excuses exempt consequences. A lazy professor, tenderhearted parent, do-good judge, or kindly supervisor may give us what we want if we have a good excuse. Then, life happens. We are faced with situations in which excuses don't work.

We may have very good reasons why we have never quit smoking, but our doctors can't exempt us from the pain, suffering, and death from lung cancer. An alcoholic may point out that it is heredity that causes his excess drinking, but his liver doesn't care for his excuses. We may have good reasons for not making payments on a car loan, but banks can't afford to accept excuses in place of loan payments. If they did, they'd make more delinquent loans than good ones and go out of business.

We may have good reasons for not keeping our marriage together, but these excuses are poor substitutes for the stable family life that our kids deserve. We may have great excuses for our failure to perform at work. However, until our employers can pay their bills with our excuses, they will either fire us or go broke listening to our excuses.

One afternoon, I realized how futile it really is to make excuses. I was speaking on this very topic the next day, so it was heavy on my mind. I was driving along in my car, deep in thought on the futility of making excuses, when I heard a ding. I looked down and my dash read "25 Miles to Empty."

As I said, I was deep in thought. I didn't bother myself with the "distance to empty" gauge until it dinged again. This time I only had ten miles until empty. "Oops," I said, "I forgot." I had an excuse for not stopping to get gas. I had more important things to think about, and it slipped my mind again. I decided I would fill up right after I made a quick stop at the store. Unfortunately, the lines were a lot longer than usual and there were only two checkout stands open. Now I had an even better excuse. It wasn't my fault the store was crowded and the management didn't have enough checkout lines open. Now that I was running late, I had a really great excuse for not taking the time to stop and get gas. Great excuse. Legitimate excuse. But how many extra miles did that excuse get me? Zero.

I did make it to the gas station with "4 Miles to Empty" flashing on my dashboard. Just as I arrived at the pump, up came this massive thunderstorm with blowing rain. I thought, "I can't get out in this mess. I'll get soaked." Yet another great excuse, but unless I wanted to walk home in the rain, I had better get gas. My car accepts gas, not excuses. Truth was, one gallon of gas at the pump was worth more than the very best excuse I could come up with. I ended up arriving at my next stop late and soaking wet, but my car got its gas. Why? Because my car would not accept my excuses.

Unfortunately, life is a lot more like my car than a lazy college professor. Excuses are futile. They don't work. Seldom do they change our consequences, so we should not get into the habit of using them. We can't afford deluding ourselves into thinking that excuses will make everything okay. Instead, we should spend the time working on making sure we don't need an excuse.

FEELING GOOD ISN'T ALWAYS GOOD

The other reason we give excuses is to make ourselves feel better when we fail. I feel a lot better about being a loser if I can blame someone or something else for my losses. The problem is that no matter who's to blame, I am still the loser.

Coming up with a great excuse is easy. With a little creativity, any of us can find a gazillion things beyond our control that will explain why our life stinks. There is the government, teachers, bad luck, parents, taxes, the boss, corporate America, genetics, fate, the stars, a spouse, kids, age, race, height, poor health, a lousy hometown, the economy, and circumstances. These are great excuses to ease the pain. The problem is that even after making all these great excuses, your life still stinks.

We use excuses as a painkiller. A painkiller is okay unless it masks a dangerous underlying disease. If I have a headache, I may take an aspirin and feel better. If that aspirin keeps me from going to the doctor and discovering I have a brain tumor, then it is bad for me in the long run.

Excuses are emotional painkillers. Unfortunately, the pain they kill is usually telling us that something needs to change in our life. Kill the pain, and we kill the motivation to fix our life.

Here's a simple truth. Losing should hurt. We want it to hurt. We should never avoid the hurt that goes along with losing. Our goal should never to become a good loser. If we become a good loser, we become good at it. We can become such great losers that we do it every time. It is better to go through painful losses and eventually become a winner than to be comfortable losing and spend our lives as losers.

That doesn't mean that we should be obnoxious losers. An obnoxious loser cries, screams, blames teammates, cusses at the reporter, hates the coach, begs to be traded, punches a hole in the locker room wall, and then goes home and kicks the dog.

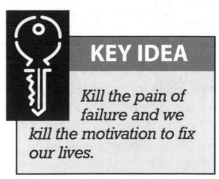

KEY IDEA

Kill the pain of failure and we kill the motivation to fix our lives.

We never want to do that. We should be graceful when we lose. Congratulate the winners. Tell the reporters how well the opponents played. Search for what we could have done to prepare better. Then, when we are alone, cry because it hurts. Nurture the hurt so that it pushes us to work harder. That is how to be a graceful loser, not a good one.

I didn't let my children play in a particular basketball league this past year because they didn't keep score. Why? Because life keeps score. The officials running the league didn't want the children to get upset if they lost. So? I want my children to hurt when they lose. I want them to learn to handle losing in a graceful way. I don't want losing to hurt so bad they won't play. But I want them to keep score, and when they lose, I want them to feel the sting of defeat. As I said, life keeps score. There are winners and there are losers. We must not let our excuses turn us into losers.

ACCEPTING RESPONSIBILITY

Excuses don't work. The best they can do is make us feel good when we shouldn't feel good. So, we must avoid them. In fact, we must do the exact opposite. We must take full responsibility for our actions.

The single best measure of our maturity is the extent to which we accept responsibility for where we are and what we do. I may be ninety-nine years old, but if I don't take full responsibility for my actions, I am still immature. A child of ten who has learned to accept responsibility is showing a great deal more maturity than many of the adults I know. Children are given privileges based on the amount of responsibility they can handle. If we use responsibility as an indication of how mature our children are, then isn't it also a good indication of our own maturity?

KEY IDEA

The best measure of our maturity is the extent to which we accept responsibility for where we are and what we do.

There is no difference between a child and an adult when things are going their way. Adults and children alike are happy and satisfied when everything is going well. The difference between someone who is mature and someone who is not can only be seen when things aren't going well. Maturity takes responsibility. Immaturity makes excuses.

Patti was a part-time student in one of my night classes. During the day, she worked full time as a secretary for a government agency. Though she was in her mid-twenties, she still lived at home with her parents.

One evening when I gave an exam, Patti was the last student to turn in her test. She was crying. "I flunked this exam," she sniffled. Judging from all the blank spaces where answers were supposed to be, I could see she was right. I couldn't understand why she took so long to write so little, but given that she was already crying, I didn't think it was a good time to ask.

"You know why I flunked this exam?" Patti said. "It's my parents. Why wouldn't I flunk? Every day, they tell me how stupid I am. They think I can't do anything. They tell me there is no use in my going to college. I am too stupid to graduate. How can I do anything when I hear that every night?"

The solution seemed obvious to me. Here was a twenty-five-year-old single woman with no children and a full-time government job living at home. "If your parents are keeping you down, then move out."

"I can't," she said. "There is no way I can afford to live on my own."

"Patti, does every single woman like yourself who is making the same money you are have to live at home? Can no one in your financial situation afford to live on their own? Does every single person like you live with her parents?"

"I don't know," she answered.

"Come on Patti," I said. "You can't leave this question blank, too." Then I repeated the question.

"I guess there are people who live on their own, but I just don't know how they do it," she responded.

"That's your job," I said. "Your job is to figure out how they do it."

"I just couldn't," she replied, shaking her head.

"You don't have to move out" I said. "That's your choice. But if you choose to stay home, quit acting like the dog on the nail."

"What dog on a nail?" she asked.

"It's an old joke salespeople tell," I said. The story goes like this:

There was a salesperson who got lost down an old country back road. He stopped at a farmer's house to get directions. While he was talking to the farmer, a lazy old hound dog lying on the porch raised its head and howled. The dog sounded as though he were in real pain. The dog did that every minute or so. Finally, the salesperson asked what was wrong with the dog.

"He's lying on a nail and it hurts," the farmer answered.

"So why doesn't he get up and move?" the salesperson asked.

The farmer thought for a minute and said, "I guess it hurts bad enough to howl about it but not bad enough to do something about it."

"Patti," I said, "if you stay at home, quit complaining. Accept that you have chosen to live with your negative parents and resign yourself to the consequences of your choice. On the other hand, if you don't want your growth to be totally stifled by your negative parents, then move out. Either way, quit blaming and making excuses. Get up and move or quit howling about the pain."

That was harsh, but I think it shocked her into seeing that she was indeed failing to accept responsibility for her own life. She did very well the rest of the semester and actually ended up making a good grade in the class. More importantly, I could see her outlook on life begin to change. The last day of the semester, she said she still wasn't sure exactly what she would do, but that she was at least looking for the best way to rearrange things in her life.

TESTING OUR EXCUSES

I gave Patti a way to judge her excuses that is not quite as strict as the Fig Tree Standard. Do others in my circumstances overcome the challenges I am facing? If so, then those challenges aren't roadblocks. They are obstacles. If we blame obstacles, we are making excuses.

If we say that we are too young, we should ask ourselves if anyone younger than we are has ever attained what we want. The son of a friend of mine was awarded two Ph.D.'s from the most prestigious institution in our state before he turned twenty years old. So, ask yourself, "Am I really too young to pursue my dream?"

If our excuse is that we are too old, we should ask if anyone older has ever achieved what we want to do. Colonel Sanders, who founded Kentucky Fried Chicken, had an incredible rags-to-riches story. When he was sixty-seven years old, he was still in rags. All he had when he retired was an old car, a Social Security check, and a chicken recipe. He drove all over the Southeast promoting his chicken. He went from broke to a multi-millionaire because he refused to use poverty and old age as excuses.

Another common excuse is that we are not qualified. Here is the question to ask. Has anyone with fewer qualifications ever made himself or herself qualified for what I want to do? Not many babies are born qualified. Somewhere between birth and death we all have to become qualified for whatever we do. People aren't born with qualifications. They earn them.

If our excuse is our race, we should ask ourselves if anyone from our race has ever risen above the prejudice we face and conquered something great. You don't have to look far to see people of all races accomplishing some pretty incredible things. Does the prejudice make it harder? Yes, it does. But it doesn't make it impossible, or else we wouldn't see the massive contributions people of all races are making.

Perhaps our excuse is our parents. Has anyone with parents worse than ours overcome abuse to rise to greatness? In my view, we can use the parents excuse for the first twenty years of our life, but the next sixty years is up to us.

Are we physically challenged in some way? It doesn't take long to find someone like Helen Keller. Can you hear? Can you see? If so, you are further along than she was.

How about our circumstances? Can we blame them? Again, has anyone ever come from worse circumstances than ours to achieve great things? Statistics show that an immigrant arriving in the United States without a penny and not knowing a soul is more likely to become a millionaire than someone who was born here. Why? Immigrants are looking for opportunities, not excuses, so many of them leap over obstacles like a deer over a log.

WHEN WE QUIT MAKING EXCUSES

Jim Rohn is an example of a person who realized just how shallow his excuses were when he was first starting out in business. Most people who have studied success have been inspired by Jim Rohn's teachings. However, he didn't start out too strong on his success journey. In fact, when he was twenty-five years old, his life was going nowhere. He was behind on his promises. He had pennies in his pockets and creditors at his door. He had been working hard for six years and he had nothing whatsoever to show for it.

That's when he met a man who would change his life. The man's name was Earl Shoaff. Mr. Shoaff asked Jim Rohn a simple question. "How are you doing?" Jim Rohn said he wasn't doing very well, and Mr. Shoaff replied, "I suggest you don't do that any more."

Jim Rohn came out with a long list of excuses for his problems in life. He blamed the government. He blamed the economy. He blamed taxes. He blamed the banks. He blamed employers. He blamed his negative relatives.

Mr. Shoaff didn't buy any of Jim Rohn's excuses. "I know people who are doing quite well. They face the same economy you do. They deal with the same banks you have to deal with. They pay even more taxes than you do. Their relatives are negative. They face all the challenges you do, and yet they are doing well. I suggest your problems aren't

KEY IDEA

If the source of our problems is within us, that's great news! That means we can immediately go to work solving them.

with everyone and everything you are blaming. I suggest that your problem is with you."

Jim Rohn realized that Mr. Shoaff was right. Others faced the same challenges he did, yet they weren't broke. They didn't have creditors at their doorstep. They weren't breaking their promises. The problem wasn't with all the things Rohn was blaming. The problem was with himself. He described the feeling that this realization gave him in one word: "Trauma."

Once the trauma settled down, Jim Rohn began to get excited. He realized if the problems were out there, he didn't have much hope of changing them. The government wasn't going to change. The banks weren't going to change. Taxes weren't going to change. On the other hand, if the problem was with himself, he could do something about that. He could go to work on that immediately.

Mr. Shoaff gave Mr. Rohn a challenge. He said, "You've been working for six years and have nothing to show for it. I suggest that you set a goal that, six years from now, you'll have a million dollars."

Mr. Shoaff then went on to explain why he should set the goal. The only way you make a million dollars is to be worth a million dollars. Money certainly isn't the best measure of a person's worth, but it does indicate something. We spend the majority of our waking hours working for money, and if the result of all this work is that we are dead broke, then something must be wrong. At that point, Jim Rohn was not worth a million dollars, or he would have had a million dollars.

Jim Rohn took the challenge. He immediately went to work on himself, and the next six years of his life were totally different. In that time, he became a millionaire. The person that he was also significantly improved in the process.

Here's what Jim Rohn observed about those six years. The government didn't change. Taxes didn't change. The banks didn't change. The economy didn't change. His negative relatives didn't change. None of the things that he blamed for his lot in life changed. It was he who changed, and when he did, his life changed.

Jim Rohn's life changed when his thinking changed. He saw the possibilities in life, and he stopped making excuses. "You can make money or you can make excuses" goes the popular saying. "You just can't make both at the same time."

The option to change our lives by changing our thinking is open to all of us. Each of us can live an incredible life filled with fun and fulfillment. We don't have to wait for someone to fix the world before we do. We need only fix our own thinking.

It starts when we see the incredible possibilities that lie before us. We know we are adopting right thinking when we stop making excuses and start accepting full responsibility for our lives. At that point, an incredible thing happens. We step out and move forward in life. That's the next key to unlocking the door to success.

KEY 4

Heaven never helps the person who will not act.
—Sophocles

INITIATIVE: FAVOR ACTION OVER ENDLESS CONTEMPLATION

When Michael Eisner took over as CEO of Disney, the company was struggling. It was worth about $2 billion. After fifteen years under Eisner, the company was dominating the entertainment industry and was worth almost $100 billion.

A couple years after Eisner joined Disney, an idea began being tossed around. Some executives thought that the company could open up its own chain of retail stores carrying a wide variety of Disney merchandise. There were other executives who thought that was a bad idea. Both sides had their arguments as to why Disney stores would or would not work. The idea of a retail store became a hot topic for discussion around Disney corporate headquarters for months.

Eventually, Eisner saw the foolishness of letting this debate consume his team of corporate executives. Rather than figuring out whether or not it would be a good idea, Eisner simply took action. It wouldn't cost that much to rent a store at a local mall and stock it full of merchandise. If people shopped there, then it was a good idea. If they did not, then they would be out a few months' operating expenses for a store at a mall. Certainly a multibillion-dollar corporation could afford that.

So that's what they did. On March 28, 1987, they opened their first store at a mall in Glendale, California. It was an immediate hit, so Disney started opening more and more stores. Now, there are almost seven hundred Disney Stores worldwide. Annually, 250 million people visited these stores.

Eisner practiced the fourth key to all success. He favored action over endless contemplation. I don't know if anyone at Disney realized just how profitable these stores would become. However, I am sure that

Eisner realized that all the debate in the world wouldn't make Disney one dollar of profit.

When I teach marketing research, my students are surprised at how I start the class. I spend the first week of the semester showing them how to decide whether or not to even do marketing research. They come into class thinking that it is always wise to do more research. Not so.

Same goes for all of us. Every day, we face decisions on whether to act or not. Sometimes we go ahead and take action. Sometimes we do nothing at all. Sometimes we spend our time thinking about what we should do. How we make our decisions has a big impact on our success. So how do we decide whether to act, think, or walk away?

HOW DO WE DECIDE?

In theory, here's how we should make our decision. First, we should look at the upside potential. What do we have if things turned out right? Then we should look at the downside risk. How are we hurt if everything goes wrong? Then we should try to guess the chances of these two things happening. If the upside potential is worth the downside risk, then we should go ahead and act. If not, then we don't. We only do more analysis if it helps us improve our decision-making. Quite often, it does not.

Going back to the Disney Store example, that's how Eisner made his decision. He looked at the upside potential. They had the potential to make millions upon millions of dollars. He looked at the downside risk. If not one single customer showed up, they would only be out the costs of running a mall store for a few months. He looked at the likelihood of success. Since some of his very smart executives thought it would work, the chances of success seemed good. Put in those terms, the decision was easy to make.

Eisner risked thousands of dollars for a good chance at making hundreds of millions. For Disney, that was an easy call. It would be nice if all of our decisions were that easy to make. Unfortunately, they are not. Things are seldom that clear-cut. Seldom

KEY IDEA

We all favor either acting, analyzing, or walking away. When we have to decide, we will do whichever of these we favor.

do we have so much to gain and so little to lose. Oftentimes, we don't know what to do.

When things aren't so clear, how do we decide? Some of us tend to do nothing. Any time an opportunity comes our way, we automatically think it won't work. Others of us like to gather more information and think about it. We easily become victims of "analysis paralysis." Then there are those who like to take action. These are the ones who tend to see the possibilities and are willing to take reasonable risks.

WHICH BIAS IS BEST?

We all have our own biases. We have a bias toward action, toward analysis, or toward doing nothing. We usually decide in a way that is consistent with our own bias. Is one of these biases better than the other two? Absolutely!

Two of the most influential books written in the last quarter of the twentieth century were *In Search of Excellence* by Tom Peters and Robert Waterman and *The 7 Habits of Highly Effective People* by Stephen Covey. *In Search of Excellence* became the best selling business book of all time. *The 7 Habits of Highly Effective People* spent years on the best sellers list.

Both of these books looked at success, but they studied it in different arenas. *In Search of Excellence* looked at success in business. *The 7 Habits of Highly Effective People* looked at personal success. The approach they took to study success was the same. They both took a huge amount of information and condensed it all down to a few simple principles.

Peters and Waterman studied hundreds upon hundreds of companies and tried to see what made the truly excellent ones different from all the rest. They identified fewer than a dozen traits that are common to all excellent companies. Covey distilled over two hundred years of personal development writings down to a mere seven habits. The fascinating thing about these two books is this: Though they looked at success in different arenas, they both discovered that the starting point for success is the same.

Peters and Waterman call it a "bias for action." They say that all the other characteristics of successful companies stem from this one trait. When forced to choose between the risks of action and the comfort of doing nothing, successful companies choose to step out and take action. Less successful companies choose comfort.

Covey noted the same thing about individuals. His first habit of highly successful people is that they are "proactive." They see what needs to be done and they do it. Less successful people are reactive or, worse, inactive. They either let their emotions drive them or they do nothing at all.

Whether we are seeking success in business or in our private lives, we must have an action orientation. As Covey says, we will act or we will be acted upon. As Peters and Waterman point out, we either seize opportunities by taking action, or we miss our window of opportunity.

ACTION MEANS SUCCESS

Indeed, life rewards action and not endless contemplation. We must make sure our thoughts are always leaning toward action. In all situations, we must be figuring out what we can do to move forward. Unfortunately, it is often biased toward doing nothing.

KEY IDEA

Our thoughts should always lean toward action. In all situations, we must figure out what we can do to move forward.

Why? It goes back to the first key to success. We are where we are in life because of how we think. To be constantly moving forward, we must make the connection in our mind between action and success. Instead, we make the wrong connections. We think stability means security. We think activity means progress. We think urgent means important. We think that the right time is when everything is just right. We think that courageous means fearless.

Any one of these wrong connections can keep us from our goals. Together, they can have a devastating effect on our success. So let's spend some time seeing how we can disconnect ourselves from some very dangerous thinking.

STABILITY DOESN'T MEAN SECURITY

We are at a fascinating time in human history. The world is changing. Our lives are improving. Still, we long for stability. Progress is change and yet change challenges our spirit.

For most of human existence, the key to survival was constancy, not innovation. Our ancient ancestors concentrated on learning and passing along time-honored traditions. The challenge was to figure out how to do things exactly like the previous generation did them. The time it took for an innovation to occur could be measured in generations, not months or years.

Farmers didn't re-invent farming every five years. They practiced it exactly like they learned it. To do anything different might result in a crop failure that could totally wipe them out. A blacksmith didn't change the way metal was formed every few months. The same methods were passed down from generation to generation.

Life is no longer that way. Stability is a thing of the past. To do things like they have always been done is fatal. I tell my students that all the technology they learn in college is likely to be totally obsolete five years after they graduate. Security now comes through an ability to change with the times.

KEY IDEA

The real dangers in today's world lie inside our comfort zone.

Just because technology has burst onto the scene, that doesn't mean human nature has changed. In many ways, we are just like the medieval farmer and blacksmith. By nature, we get comfort from figuring out how things have always been done and doing them the same way. We still have this trait that allowed our ancient ancestors to survive.

Science moves forward. Technology moves forward. Business moves forward. Our souls cry out for things to remain the same. Change may be exciting, but it is also uncomfortable. The action that brings success is not the action that brings comfort. An action orientation will push us to do things way outside our comfort zone.

The real dangers in today's world lie inside our comfort zone. John F. Kennedy was prophetic about the world we were entering when he said, "There are risks and costs to a program of action, but they are far less than the long-range risks and costs of comfortable inaction."

One time, I heard a speaker say, "If you always do what you've always done, you'll always get what you've always gotten." That made sense so I started saying that to my students. Eventually, I realized that there was a problem with that thinking, and here is what it is.

KEY IDEA

Doing the same thing over and over works when nothing changes. Things are changing. Stability no longer means security. It means extinction.

That statement assumes that we live in a static world. It assumes that nothing changes. The problem is that things always change. For example, a winning football coach couldn't stick to the idea that if he just keeps doing what he has done, he will get what he has always gotten. Keep running up the middle, and before long, the defense will adjust and shut down the middle. No matter how successful one passing pattern is, a coach can't call it too many times, or a defensive back will "jump the route" and intercept the next pass.

Doing what you've always done because it's been successful in the past doesn't work in business either. The second you have success, there are hundreds or even of thousands of competitors trying to copy and improve on what you have done. The world changes so rapidly in business that what made you successful today will send you into bankruptcy tomorrow. That's why the book *Who Moved My Cheese?* became so popular. Managers bought it by the truckload, and handed it out to their employees. The message was things will change, whether you like it or not. We can either change or die. And it took a silly little story about two mice and two men to help people see that. Keep doing what you're doing, and, eventually, you're left wondering what happened to all the things you have come to enjoy in life.

Change happens in all areas of our lives, so to survive, we must take new approaches and use new strategies. When we don't take new action, the competition adjusts. The world changes. Something unexpected happens, such as the invention of the Internet, and we start getting smacked doing the very thing that once worked. Refusing to step out and take action may give us a feeling of stability. But stability no longer means security. In today's world, it means extinction.

ACTIVITY DOESN'T MEAN PROGRESS

One time, some researchers asked a large group of managers whether or not they took initiative. They all felt that they did. These researchers then asked these managers what they felt it meant to take initiative. The average and low-performing managers talked about getting things fixed when they broke, answering the phone when the secretary was out, and the like. The highly successful managers saw these things as routine. Doing them was just part of the job. Taking initiative meant doing much more.

These researchers discovered something that is very important for us to know. Activity doesn't mean progress. Just because we are doing something doesn't mean we are moving forward.

KEY IDEA

The best way to avoid taking initiative is to stay busy.

The best way to avoid taking initiative is to stay busy but unproductive. Busyness is the worst form of laziness because it makes us feel good but it doesn't move us toward our goals. At least when we are on the couch doing nothing, we know we are being lazy. However, when we are zipping around doing all kinds of unimportant things, we actually feel productive. We let our activity ease our minds as we avoid doing what must be done.

I have always had this problem when it comes to grading. I hate grading papers, so it is amazing how busy I can be when I have exams sitting on my desk. A while back I was grading finals when my daughter Alice told me that she saw a big fish tank complete will all accessories for sale. I had been talking about getting myself a nice fish tank for twenty years, but I never did. It takes a lot of work to get one of those big tanks up and running, so I never bought one. However, this time I went for it.

Lisa asked me why I finally bought the tank I had talked about for so many years. I could have said it was a good price or just the right tank. I could have said that I was particularly attracted to the fish. All these were true. However, I had to be honest with her, so I told her that if I hadn't had all those finals to grade, I would have never even looked at it.

I can't feel good about putting off grading by playing basketball, going to the movies, or kicking back in the recliner. But I don't feel guilty at all when I am nice and busy "working." I stay busy doing unimportant things so I can avoid doing what I don't want to do. Knowing me, I will probably clean the tank at regular intervals—every time I have exams waiting to be graded.

KEY IDEA

If our hours are filled and yet we are no better off today than we were yesterday, then something is wrong. Are we making progress or are we just staying busy?

Some salespeople get great at staying busy to avoid making sales. They take prime selling time and use it to alphabetize their business cards and sort their paper clips. Their company may need new customers, but, because of call reluctance, they keep calling on existing accounts. They won't be found sleeping late or going to the movies in the afternoon because their conscience wouldn't let them. So they run around busily doing unimportant things of marginal value. They feel good because they are busy. Their company suffers because they aren't productive.

When managers get into this trap, it can be deadly. A company's downfall can be when its managers use planning and organizing as a way to avoid acting. Calling meetings to avoid tackling the difficult issues can have a devastating effect. Not only are the managers avoiding what they need to be doing, they are also pulling their people away from what they should be doing.

Running the numbers can be another particularly bad form of busyness. Analysis is only useful if it helps us take reasonable risks. Gathering information and engaging in analysis beyond that is simply a way to avoid taking risks and moving into action. Life doesn't reward endless analysis. It rewards us when we actually do something with our analysis.

People who are going places have a full schedule. However, not all those with full schedules are going places. If our hours are filled and yet we are no better off today than we were yesterday, something is wrong. We need to see if we are inclined toward action or simply satisfied with busyness. Otherwise, we will be no better than the person sitting in the rocking chair—a lot of movement but no progress.

URGENT DOESN'T MEAN IMPORTANT

A third great killer of action is procrastination. What is procrastination? Here is a great definition:

Procrastination is being driven by urgency and not importance.

I watch my students fall victim to procrastination every semester. At the start of every semester, they get their term project assignments. They remember the end-of-the-term crunch from last semester, and the semester before that, and the semester before that …. So they commit to going ahead and knocking the projects out early in the term.

There's a lot of stuff you can't anticipate when making a commitment like that. For example, how can you know that the guys will put together a great basketball game right when you were planning to go to the library? Who could tell that television would be so good on the exact night you wanted to organize your research? You can't

KEY IDEA

Procrastination makes us live our lives under the tyranny of the urgent.

turn your back on your fraternity or sorority when they need you. You can't ignore your boyfriend or girlfriend. Then there's that special chance to hitch a ride to the ski slopes or the beach. Opportunities like that don't come along every day, and you certainly can't pass them up. And if that's not enough, who would have expected our team to make it to the playoffs? No way can we miss that game!

Students understand the importance of the term project. However, when they are procrastinating, they aren't responding to importance. They are responding to urgency. But urgency doesn't arrive until about two weeks before the end of the term. Then, it hits them between the eyes that they have to get some things done or they will fail. They stay up all night writing. They live on caffeine and sugar. They become frazzled and testy.

In *The 7 Habits of Highly Effective People* mentioned earlier, Stephen Covey makes an interesting observation. He says that the most effective people respond to importance, not urgency. They seldom have to deal with the urgent because they have already taken care of it long before it became urgent. People who procrastinate live under the tyranny of the urgent. They are constantly letting important things become urgent, so they are always under stress.

Whenever people find out all of the things I am doing in my professional and personal life, they automatically assume that my life is filled with stress. It is not, and here's why. I manage my time very closely, focusing on the important tasks before they become urgent. One of the best things I have ever done to improve my quality of life is to develop

KEY IDEA

Many important things never become urgent. If we only respond to urgency, these important things never get done.

a time management system. With it, I do important things before they become urgent. That way, I can enjoy my filled-to-the-brim life rather than be stressed out by it. Until we learn to respond to importance rather than urgency, our lives will always be stressed.

However, the biggest problem with procrastination is not the stress it creates. It is the things that it leaves out of our lives. Some of the most important things in life never become urgent. If all we respond to is the urgent, these important things never get done.

I recently had a student named Kim. She was a mother of three who went back to school after sitting out for several years. She told the class that for years she would drive by the university every day and think, "I need to go back to school." But she would just keep driving. One day, she realized something. Right in her back yard she had an opportunity to get a very good university education that could take her places she wasn't going. She was letting it slip away.

I'll never forget what she told the class. "One day I realized the school administrators weren't going to throw a degree into the back seat of my car as I drove by. I had to do something to earn it. The time wasn't right, but it never would be right. So that day, rather than driving by, I stopped. I enrolled. It was tough balancing a family and an education, but I am so glad I did because in two weeks I graduate."

The semester she decided to go back to school was the semester that changed her life. As a wife and mother of three, there were many urgent things she needed to do. Getting an education wasn't one of them. There would always be next semester and, if not then, the next semester after that. It wasn't until Kim decided to respond to the important rather than the urgent that she started to improve her life.

THE RIGHT TIME DOESN'T MEAN EVERYTHING IS JUST RIGHT

One of the things Kim had to realize was that the perfect time would never come. She told us that, when her kids were small, she thought,

"The time isn't right. I will wait until the kids get older." Then the kids got older. She realized that it might have been easier to go back to school when the kids were younger. One reason we don't step out and take action is that we are waiting for the perfect time and the perfect situation to begin.

KEY IDEA

Get moving and make repairs as you go.
—Josh Gordon

Circumstances will never be just right. The time will never be just right. The right time and place to get started is now. I was recently speaking at a religious gathering. I told the audience that Satan doesn't need to get us to say, "no." He only needs to get us to say, "tomorrow."

In one of my classes, I had a student named Josh. He was reading the autobiography of a highly successful businessman. I will never forget how Josh described the way this businessman did things. "He would take action and make repairs along the way." That's a key to success. We get started and make repairs as we go.

There is a time to wait and there is a time to take action. However, if we are waiting for things to be perfect before we take action, we will never take action. George Bernard Shaw summed up this way of thinking when he said:

"People are always blaming their circumstances for what they are. I don't believe in circumstances. The people who get on in this world are the people who get up and look for the circumstances they want, and if they can't find them, they make them."

COURAGEOUS DOESN'T MEAN FEARLESS

Often, we don't step out because we are afraid to do so. Indeed, often there are fears associated with what we want to do. We are afraid to fail. We are afraid to give up our security. We are afraid of what others may think. We are afraid that we might lose money. We are afraid that we might be demoted or fired. We are afraid of change. We may even be afraid to succeed.

We can't let our fears hold us back. Everyone has fears. Successful people move ahead in spite of their fears. Often, the very thing they fear happens. However, they achieved a great victory because

> ## KEY IDEA
>
> *All men have fears. Brave men conquer their fears and move forward—sometimes to death, but always to victory.*
> —Palace Guard, Ancient Athens

they defeated fear. That is exactly what the motto of the palace guard of ancient Athens said. Over their headquarters hung these words: "All men have fears. Brave men conquer their fears and move forward—sometimes to death, but always to victory."

Around our campus, we have a huge number of students that are called "nontraditional." That simply means that they aren't in their late teens or early twenties. For whatever reasons, they stayed out of school for a number of years before coming back. Many of them are married and have children. A lot of them work full time and go to school part time.

Every nontraditional student I ever met was afraid to go back to school. They didn't know what to expect. They didn't know if they could compete with the younger students. They didn't know what to do to get started. They didn't know if they could afford it. They didn't know what their friends would say. They didn't know if they could balance family and school. Because of that, sometimes it took years before they actually enrolled again.

Once in the classroom, they find that their fears weren't justified. They have the maturity that many of the traditional students don't have, so they usually do quite well. They find that there are many others like themselves who are returning to college in their thirties and forties. They find that they can handle the challenges.

Nelson Mandela said, "Courage isn't the absence of fear but the conquering of fear." Without fear, we cannot be courageous. It doesn't take courage to do something we aren't afraid to do. How much courage does it take to polish off a banana split? Having fears won't prevent us from succeeding. If that were so, none of us would succeed. We will have fears, but we must also have courage. Courage does not mean we don't have fear. It means we don't let our fears stop us.

DEVELOPING AN ACTION ORIENTATION

Having an action orientation is a key to all success. It is one of the most difficult keys to master. Why? It robs us of our false sense of security. It forces us to make progress and not just stay busy. It pushes us to do the important and not just the urgent. It makes us step out when things aren't exactly right. It forces us to face our fears.

KEY IDEA

Courage isn't the absence of fear but the conquering of fear.
—Nelson Mandela

That's a lot of stuff to fight. If it weren't for the great rewards that come from action, it wouldn't be worth it. But it is worth it. So where do we start? To take the right action, there is a mental puzzle we must solve and an emotional battle we must win. Let's explore each.

SOLVING THE MENTAL PUZZLE

It is a challenge figuring out how to get all the important stuff into our day. Scheduling our time is like trying to solve a puzzle. On one side, we have this endless list of things we could be doing. On the other side, we have a very limited amount of time. Specifically, we only have twenty-four hours in a day. The challenge is to fit all the important things into those twenty-four hours. The puzzle won't be solved if we try to stuff the wrong stuff into the twenty-four hours.

If we stick in too much television and not enough personal development, the puzzle can't be solved. If we spend too much time in idle conversation on meaningless topics with underachieving people, the puzzle won't be solved.

Sometimes the puzzle requires us to figure out the exact right amount of time to spend on things. Not too much, not too little. For a period of time, I played a noon basketball game. We played for two hours, three times a week. I justified it in my mind by saying I was staying in good shape.

True, my cardiovascular conditioning was awesome. However, by the time I drove to the gym, suited up, stretched out, played two hours, cooled down, showered off, got dressed, and returned to the office, I had spent over three hours. I was taking more than ten hours a week away from my family and my work for cardiovascular conditioning. That made some other parts of the puzzle not fit. I had to drop the game and find another way to stay in shape.

How well we solve this puzzle will determine how far we go in life. I heard a reporter one time criticize Ronald Reagan for the way he managed his day. "He has this to-do list. It seems like his greatest joy in life is crossing something off his to-do list. I can't imagine the President of the United States making this little to-do list and then gleefully going through his day scratching things off."

It didn't sound like such a bad idea to me. Perhaps the reporter needed to learn how to make out his own to-do list. After all, Reagan was running the nation while the reporter was working for an editor. Reagan lived in the White House and had Air Force One at his command. The reporter probably lived in a one-bedroom apartment and struggled to find a parking space for his car. Reagan made the big decisions and the reporter just wrote about them.

Reagan made it to the White House by working through a to-do list. How? I guess he must have put the right things on his to-do list, crossing them off one by one. I'd say he did a pretty good job of solving his puzzle.

If we get the right things onto our to-do list and if we do them, we might be amazed how far we can go. How do we decide what to put on our to-do list? A whole bunch of urgent things will find their way onto our list. That's just life. However, if we look at our list and all we ever have are urgent things, then something is wrong. We have to figure out a way to get some important things that aren't urgent on there, too. That's part of solving the puzzle. We must figure out how to keep our list from being taken over by urgent things or there will be no room for important things.

To do that, we first have to figure out what's important. That's the other part of the puzzle. It is extremely important that we solve this part of the puzzle first. The puzzle can't be solved until we figure out what's important and what's not.

WHAT'S IMPORTANT?

The Cheshire Cat taught this lesson to Alice as she was walking around lost in her wonderland. Alice came to a fork in the road. In the middle of the fork sat the Cheshire Cat. Looking at the cat, Alice asked, "Which road should I take?"

"Where are you going?" asked the cat.

"I don't know," answered Alice.

"Then it doesn't matter."

The cat shared with Alice one of the simplest yet most profound truths of the universe. If we don't know where we're going, then it doesn't matter which road we take. If our destination is "anywhere," then whatever road we happen to be on will get us there. As the ancient saying goes, "To the ship without a destination, no wind is a good wind."

KEY IDEA

If we don't know where we're going, then it doesn't matter which road we take.

Ronald Reagan was able to figure out what he needed to do to become president because he knew that he wanted to be president. Knowing that, he would put things on his to-do list that would make him president. Had he wanted to be a movie producer, he would have undoubtedly put different things on his list. He would have solved his puzzle in a totally different manner. What we want to do determines how we solve our puzzle.

Is it as simple as deciding what we want, and then putting the things on our to-do list that will get us there? No. There is one other component: growth. The Ronald Reagan who ran for and was elected President in 1980 wasn't the same Ronald Reagan who didn't come close to getting the Republican nomination when he ran against Richard Nixon in 1968. He wasn't the same Ronald Reagan who came close to defeating Gerald Ford for the Republican nomination in 1976.

Each time he ran for president, he learned and grew. He understood better how to solve his puzzle. He put better things on his to-do list. Not only that, he also became better at doing the things on the list. Through growth, vision, and setting the proper priorities, he solved his puzzle. He became president of the United States.

How well are we solving our puzzle? Remember the first key to all success: Judge the seed by the harvest. We can't be doing a very good job of solving our puzzle if we aren't getting what we want from life.

KEY IDEA

Successful people do the things underachievers don't want to do. Successful people don't want to do those things either, but they do them anyway.

WINNING OVER OUR EMOTIONS

Once we figure out the things we must do, we must have the emotional maturity to do them. That will always mean doing some things we don't want to do. Successful people do what underachievers don't like to do. It's not that successful people like to do them any more than underachievers. It's just that they will go ahead and do them anyway. Underachievers won't.

That is what emotional maturity is all about. It is doing the things we don't want to do because there is a reason to do so. How do we develop that kind of maturity? We do so by letting our emotions push us forward rather than hold us back.

There were two guys walking through the woods when they happened upon a big bear. One of them took off running. The other said, "What are you doing? You can't outrun a bear."

His companion said, "I don't have to outrun the bear. I only have to outrun you." One person let his fears stop him. The other put his fears behind him and got moving. Which one had the better chance for survival? The best way to deal with our fears is to let them get us moving, not to let them stop us.

PUTTING OUR FEARS BEHIND US

We should put our fears behind us rather than in front of us. If they are in front of us, they will stop us. If they are behind us, they will push us to action.

If I were out for a walk and I looked down the block and saw a vicious, snarling dog, I would stop. Why? Because the thing I fear is in front of me. On the other hand, what if the vicious dog weren't in front of me but behind me? Would I stop and wait for it to come and get me? No, the thing I fear would be behind me, so it would get me moving. If we put the things we fear in front of us, they stop us. If we put them behind us, they push us to achieve more.

The number one fear on most people's list is that of public speaking. The number two fear is death. When you go to a funeral, most people would rather be in the coffin than up giving the eulogy. Unfortunately, if we aren't willing to speak, we limit what we can accomplish.

There are two ways to deal with the fear of public speaking. One is to put it in front of us and the other is to put it behind us. If we put it in front of us, it will stop us from speaking. We will have the opportunity to speak and we will turn it down. In doing so, we limit what we can achieve.

On the other hand, we can put the fear of speaking behind us by accepting the opportunity to speak. We feel the fear but we speak anyway. Then we let our fears push us to prepare a great speech. We will do a great job because we are afraid not to. Our fears are pushing us to achieve rather than stopping us from trying.

KEY IDEA

We think that we will act when the fear goes away. That is totally backwards. The fear goes away when we act.

Here's the great part about putting our fears behind us. Eventually, they go away. Emerson said, "Do the thing you fear and the death of fear is certain." We think that, when the fear goes away, we will act. That is totally backwards. When we act, the fear goes away. The best way to conquer fear is to do the very thing we fear. Action cures fear.

When our two younger children, Allen and Alaina, were three and five years old, we visited a science museum. In the lobby was a dinosaur display, complete with a huge, twenty-foot-tall mechanical dinosaur that moved and roared. It was right in the middle of the museum. The only way to avoid it was to go behind the bookstore.

The first thing I did at the museum was walk up to the dinosaur. Allen and Alaina didn't follow Daddy. They were hiding by the bookstore with this look of terror on their faces. I knew the thing wasn't real, but they didn't. They were back there thinking, "Oh, no, Daddy's going to get gobbled up by the big green monster."

I looked at them and said, "Hey, come on over here. It's not real." They weren't convinced. It looked real to them. I let them walk behind the bookstore and I met them on the other side. Throughout the day, any time we needed to go from one part of the museum to another, we had to walk through the lobby. I would walk in front of the dinosaur and Allen and Alaina would walk behind the bookstore. However, each time, before they took the back route, they would get a little closer to the big green monster.

Finally, about two o'clock in the afternoon, Allen made a dash for it. He ran as fast as he could in front of the dinosaur. Alaina wasn't going to be left behind, so she made a dash, too. They didn't stop. They didn't look back. They just ran as fast as they could. When they got to the other side, you could see the relief on their faces that they didn't get gobbled up.

As the afternoon progressed, Allen and Alaina got more and more comfortable with Dino. By the time we left, they were dancing in front of him, saying, "You can't eat me." They had no fear whatsoever. It took time, but slowly, as they did the thing they feared, the fear disappeared.

KEY IDEA

Wisdom, not fear, should tell us what to embrace and what to shun.

We can conquer anything we fear if we just move slowly toward it. Here's how the mind works: When we face something new or different, fear is there. However, that fear diminishes as we continue being around it.

We don't need to move too fast. In fact, moving too fast can have the wrong effect. I remember seeing one dad take his little screaming kid and hold him up to the mouth of the dinosaur. That kid was thinking, "Oh, no, Daddy is feeding me to the dinosaur." I'm not sure what they call a phobia of museums, but I bet I know where it comes from. The kid may have been traumatized for life.

As long as we are patient, we cannot continue to fear the things we continue to do. It's a trait of all human beings. When we take action in the direction of our fears, eventually our fears go away. It has to happen. We are wired that way. It's in our genes.

There is a good side and a bad side to that trait of human beings. The good side is that we can use it to conquer any fear that is keeping us from achieving our purpose in life. The bad side is that we can become comfortable with something we should fear.

That's exactly how some people ruin their lives on drugs. We call it the slippery slope. A kid who has never even tasted alcohol or smoked a cigarette isn't going to say, "I think I'll give crack cocaine a try." He will try some of the "lesser" drugs. They don't kill him, so he feels comfortable with them. With less fear, he moves to harder and harder drugs. The marijuana might not kill him, but it might kill his fear of some things that can kill him.

People who are killed or injured by dangerous industrial equipment are seldom the new operators. The new people are scared of the machines, and that fear keeps them alert. However, as time goes by, the fear goes away. They no longer fear something they should be afraid of, and that's when accidents occur.

By facing our fears, we can eliminate them. By not facing them, they will remain. We must wisely choose which fears to eliminate. Some fears we should keep. We become emotionally mature as we eliminate the fears that hold us back from success.

LETTING OUR ACTIONS PROVE WE CAN

One of the most inspiring stories I have ever read was that of Heidi von Beltz. Heidi's father, Brad, was a successful Hollywood actor, and she was following in his footsteps. Then, while filming the movie *Cannonball Run*, she was in an accident that sent her shoulder through her spinal cord. The doctors told her parents that she would die in a few months. They also said that, in the few painful months that she had left to live, she would not be able to move a muscle below her neck.

In a firm voice, Brad told the doctors to say nothing of their prognosis to Heidi. He had a different plan. He would take action. He wouldn't just let his daughter waste away and die. In her book, *My Soul Purpose*, Heidi tells what it took to recover. It took years, but eventually she could stand, and with the help of a walker, even move around on her own. She didn't waste away and die as the doctors said she would. She made an incredible recovery and went on to live a fairly normal life.

What impacted me most while reading this book was the philosophy Heidi developed through her experience. If she had listened to the experts, she would have died. Her very survival can be credited to the fact that she stepped out and did some things that everyone said were foolish and futile.

She didn't really fault the doctors for thinking the way they did. After all, their opinions were based on years of accumulated research. The problem was that their research came from a form of circular logic. People who had accidents like hers were told they couldn't survive. There was nothing they could do. Because of that, they did nothing. Because they did nothing, they didn't survive. When they didn't survive, the medical community had the fact and figures that confirmed that they were right. Heidi survived because she refused to become one of their facts and figures.

She also had an interesting perspective on pain killers. She said that they didn't kill the pain. They simply killed the capacity to care about the pain. Heidi said she didn't want to kill the capacity to care about the pain. She wanted to make the pain work for her.

The Heidi von Beltz story isn't a story about one person overcoming an accident. It is a story about not giving up and taking action. Most of us don't get the results she does because we choose a different path. We think we can't achieve great things, so we don't try. Because we don't try, we are proved right. We settle for painkillers that don't really kill the pain. They just kill our capacity to feel the pain. We walk through life being a fraction of what we were meant to be. It all happens because we let idleness prove we can't succeed rather than letting actions prove we can.

It wasn't just Heidi's willingness to step out that gave her victory. There seemed to be something inside of her that refused to quit. She would set a goal and then nothing could keep her from achieving it. At one point, her goal was very modest. She simply wanted to be able to control her own flow of urine. She spent months on that one singular goal. After months of struggle, she won. It was a great victory. Imagine spending months of your life conquering something so simple that we all take for granted.

Heidi got on the road to success because she was willing to step out and take action. Her victory came because she persevered. Stepping out of our comfort zone and taking action is a key to success. However, it is of little use without the next key to success. Let's turn the page and start to explore the key of perseverance.

Key 5

*Persistence is the hard work you do after you get
tired of doing the hard work you already did.*
—Newt Gingrich

Perseverance: Be Persistent But Not Stubborn

It was half time and the coach's team was down by twenty points. He needed to make a speech to inspire his players stick to in there and not quit. Here's what he said:

"Did the Wright Brothers quit?" he yelled.

"No, they didn't," his team shouted.

"Did Abraham Lincoln quit?"

"No, he didn't."

"Did Thomas Edison quit?"

"No, he didn't."

"Did Michael Jordan quit?"

"No, he didn't."

"Did Nate Mizersky quit?" The team gave the coach a puzzled look. "I asked if Nate Mizersky quit," he yelled.

"Coach," one of the players replied. "We don't know who Nate Mizersky is."

"Of course you don't," the coach barked. "He quit."

If We Don't Quit, It's Ours

Life doesn't give much to quitters. On the other hand, life has yet to figure out how to withhold anything from the person who refuses to quit. As Benjamin Disraeli, prime minister of Great Britain, said, "Nothing can resist the person who will stake his very existence on a cause." As long as we are growing, if we persist, we will get whatever we set out for in life.

KEY IDEA

Life can't withhold anything from the person who refuses to quit.

Harland was a broke old man with nothing but a chicken recipe. He started running around trying to find someone to buy it. He got hundreds of nos before he got his first yes. He talked to more than a thousand restaurant owners, and he still hadn't broken the hundred dollar mark in chicken recipe sales.

Anyone in their right mind would have quit way before then. How many hundreds of nos in a row would it take before you started seriously doubting whether you would ever reach your chicken recipe sales dreams? But Harland Sanders wouldn't quit and, eventually, the man we know as Colonel Sanders did sell his recipe. His Kentucky Fried Chicken made him millions upon millions. His success came because he refused to quit. He refused to take no for an answer.

If we decide that we want something, and we commit to never quitting until we have it, then it is done. It is ours. We can relax and go about the work of getting it. Sure, there will be problems along the way, but we can know with absolute certainty that we will eventually have what it is that we seek if we refuse to quit and we continue to grow.

WHAT DO WE GET FROM LIFE?

I have heard it said that life will give us what we desire if we just want it badly enough. Not necessarily. Certainly desire motivates us, but I have seen many people stop short of their heart's desire. No matter how bad we want something, if we don't persevere, we won't get it. We will become a frustrated victim of unwilling desire. We will fall into the trap of thinking that desire is bad because we didn't get what we wanted. It wasn't desire that frustrated us. It was quitting short of our desire.

We know life won't give us fairness. Our fathers told us that growing up. We would say, "That's not fair" and they would say, "Life's not fair." I remember hearing that so many times growing up that I swore I would never say it to my children. However, the first time my child said, "That's not fair," guess what I said. I think that there must be something in the genes of the males of our species that makes us instinctively respond,

"Life's not fair." At least we're speaking the truth. Life isn't fair. We can't expect to get something just because it fits our idea of fairness.

Life also won't give us what we deserve. We don't have to look very far to find people who are getting a lot more from life than what they deserve. The guy who stops by the quick mart on his way home to pick up a six-pack and some cigarettes and happens to buy the winning lottery ticket is getting a lot more than he deserves. The good loving mother whose A-student child is killed by a drunk driver isn't getting what she deserves. Life doesn't give us what we deserve.

If life doesn't give us what we want, what's fair, or what we deserve, then what does it give us? Life gives us what we will settle for. As soon as we decide we want something, life will test us to see how serious we are about getting it. It will start throwing unexpected obstacles in our way. These trials are life's way of seeing what we will settle for. Life wants to know if we will settle for less than we desire. If we will, then it doesn't have to give us what we want. However, if we refuse to quit, life eventually gives up and gives us whatever it is we are pursuing.

KEY IDEA

What do we get from life? Not what we want. Not what we deserve. Not what's fair. Life gives us what we will settle for.

One time, Henry Ford decided he wanted an eight-cylinder engine cast out of a single block. He presented the problem to his engineers, who promptly told him it couldn't be done. They said it was impossible.

Ignoring what they said, Ford told them to go to work on it right away. Impossible doesn't mean much to the person who said, "Whether you think you can or you think you can't, you're right."

"Why would we want to go to work on a project that is doomed to fail?" they asked.

"Because if you don't," Ford responded, "I will fire you and hire some engineers that will work on it."

"We'll get on it right away," they said. Every week or two, the engineers would meet with Ford trying to convince him that it is impossible to cast eight cylinders out of a single block. Ford would simply tell them to get back to work on it.

Finally, after this went on for a few months, someone on the engineering team got an idea. They had been trying to put all eight cylinders in a straight line. What if they moved them side by side in a slant? They tried it and it worked. They invented the V-8 engine. One of the biggest breakthroughs in the history of the automotive industry might never have occurred if Henry Ford had let his engineers tell him it couldn't be done. Henry Ford wouldn't settle for less, so he got what he wanted.

KEY IDEA

The rewards in life come from finishing something, not starting it. We can't cross the finish line if we keep going back to the starting line.

Life tests us to see what we will settle for. If we pass the test, we get our desires. The reason life gives so few of us what we want is that most of us don't pass the test. We decide we want something. We pursue it until life throws an obstacle our way. We quit that pursuit and find something else we want. We continue with that direction until it gets tough. Then we find something else. This cycle continues. We start, quit, and start something new.

The rewards in life come from finishing something, not starting it. We never finish anything because we keep starting something new. We can't cross the finish line if we keep going back to the starting line. We may eventually give up pursuing anything at all because we never get anything we want. The dreamer becomes a do-nothing. The whole problem can be traced to quitting before the victory is won.

Does perseverance give us what we want every single time? No, just *almost* every single time. On the other hand, quitting works none of the time. As a race car driver once observed, "In order to finish first, you must first finish."

THE PARABLE OF SPLAT!

My absolute favorite story that I tell my students is the Parable of SPLAT! It is the story of the young man who went to the wise elder of the village and asked him where success is.

The elder pointed down a particular road and said, "Success is that way." Excited, the young man went running off down the road toward success. A little ways down the road came a sound: SPLAT! The kid was squashed.

Bruised and battered, the young man came staggering back to the wise man. "Where did you say success is?"

The elder pointed down the same road. The young man headed off down the road a second time. He got to the exact same spot in the road and again: SPLAT!

Crushed, the young man crawled back to the elder. "I thought you said success is down that road," the young man said.

"It is," the elder replied. "Right on the other side of SPLAT!"

All we desire in life is waiting for us, right on the other side of SPLAT. The problem is that we do exactly what the young man in the parable did. We hit SPLAT!, and rather than going on to claim our victory, we turn around and come back.

QUITTING JUST SHORT

Ross Perot once commented on how close many people are to victory when they quit. He said:

"Most people give up just when they're about to achieve success. They quit on the one-yard line. They give up at the last minute of the game, one foot from a winning touchdown."

In his classic book *Think and Grow Rich*, Napoleon Hill tells a story of this exact thing happening to a man named R. U. Darby.

Back in the gold rush days, Mr. Darby had an uncle who found gold. He staked his claim, made his map, buried his find, and went back to Maryland for the resources he needed to dig a gold mine. This uncle got Mr. Darby, along with all of his money, to go out to Colorado with him. They bought some digging equipment and went after it. They had some success, but the gold quickly disappeared. They

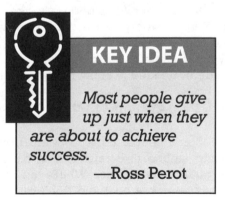

KEY IDEA

Most people give up just when they are about to achieve success.

—Ross Perot

dug and dug but to no avail. Eventually, they quit. They sold their claim and all their equipment at salvage prices. They went home broke.

The person who bought the claim and equipment took over where they left off. He dug a mere three feet and hit a vein of gold worth millions upon millions of dollars. Mr. Darby and his uncle quit just three feet short of gold.

Fortunately, Mr. Darby learned his lesson. He went on to become one of the most successful insurance salesmen in the country. He said that every time he thought of giving up, he remembered the time he quit just three feet short of gold. That big mistake taught him about perseverance, and the lesson made him a very wealthy man.

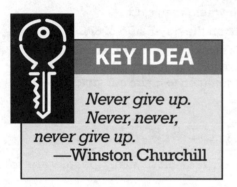

KEY IDEA

Never give up.
Never, never,
never give up.
—Winston Churchill

How often do we make the exact same mistake? Life tests us. We want something, so it throws things in our path to see if we are serious. Then, just when life is about to give in, we quit. Life says, "I'll throw one more thing at them, and then I'll give them what they want." That's when we quit.

Winston Churchill gave one of the shortest speeches in the history of the world. He was asked to speak at the academy he attended as a teen. The master of the academy told the students to pay close attention because one of the greatest orators England ever produced was about to make a speech that would go down in history.

It did. Churchill stood up, looked at the students, and said, "Never give up. Never, never, never give up." Then he sat down. That was the whole speech. Those are perhaps the most widely quoted words Winston Churchill ever spoke. I guess that's all Churchill thought the students needed to know. Never give up. Be persistent. Persevere.

PERSEVERANCE IS NOT STUBBORNNESS

Some people think they are being persistent when they are just being stubborn. Persistence is a key to success. Stubbornness can be fatal to our success. What's the difference? Persistence is when we continue after a goal and don't quit until we achieve it. We may need to try many different things to achieve the goal, but we keep going after it.

Stubbornness, on the other hand, is when we keep doing the same thing over and over. It doesn't mean we are getting closer to our goal. It just means we are unwilling to try something new. Let me borrow from nature to illustrate the difference between perseverance and stubbornness by giving you my version of the birds and the bees.

THE BIRDS AND THE BEES

My school office is a great place to write. I have a corner office on the second floor with two huge windows overlooking large grassy areas filled with trees, birds, and squirrels. The grounds crews take great care of these areas so they always look nice. In the distance, there is a shady stream with all its flowers, vines, and bushes as a backdrop. On nice days, I throw open both windows to get a cross breeze. It's the closest place to heaven on earth I've ever found.

Every now and then, I have a visitor come flying in my window. It might be a fly, a wasp, or a bee. Because my windows are so big, I even occasionally have a bird come visit me.

I keep a cup and a piece of cardboard in my filing cabinet to catch the bees and help them escape. Why? Because they will go to where there is glass and try to get out that way. Bam, they hit the glass. That didn't work, so they try it again and again. They will keep crashing into the same pane of glass over and over until they beat their little brains out. Just a few feet away there is a wide-open window, but they never find it. They are too busy trying the same route over and over. That's not persistence. That's being stubborn.

When birds end up in my office, they don't stay long. They may crash into the glass once

KEY IDEA

Perseverance doesn't mean doing the same thing over and over. It means sticking with a goal even if we need to try different things to achieve it.

or twice, but they keep trying different routes until they find the open window. That's persistence. They don't keep trying the same old thing over and over until they beat their brains out. They just keep trying different things until they reach their goal. That's persistence.

Our problem is that we are often much more like the bees than the birds. We do the same thing over and over and settle for whatever it may give us. We may even pride ourselves for sticking in there and not quitting. However, if we are just getting our brains bashed in doing the same thing over and over, we may want to take a lesson from the bird. We don't need to change the goal. We just need to try a different approach to getting what we want.

WRITING OUR GOALS IN CONCRETE

Perseverance is when we write our goals in concrete and our plans in sand. We are uncompromising about what we want, but we are flexible about how to get it. We don't give up on our goals. However, if we have a tactic that isn't working, we are open to looking for something that will work.

KEY IDEA

Perseverance is writing our goals in concrete and our plans in sand.

Stubbornness is just the opposite. Stubbornness is when we write our plans in concrete and our goals in sand. Doing the same thing over and over isn't being persistent. It's being stubborn. That's especially true when we don't have a goal in mind. Persistence only makes sense when we have a goal that we are working toward, and we are doing whatever is legal, moral, and ethical to achieve it.

I sometimes ask my students how old you have to be to retire. They often say sixty-five. Then I tell them that it was a trick question. It doesn't take age to retire. It takes money. If they had enough money, they could retire right now. At twenty-two years of age, they probably wouldn't call it retirement. They would call it being "financially independent."

Becoming financially independent is a good goal. If we could work at helping others regardless of the money we made, we could probably make some incredible contributions to the world. However, we spend our lives working for a paycheck, and then when we are old, we retire to conquer the golf course. What a difference many young people could make if they could retire when they still had great dreams. What a difference many retired people could make if they still had the dreams they had when they were young.

If we set the goal of becoming financially independent, there are many different ways of achieving it. Two of the wealthiest men this world has ever seen are Bill Gates and Warren Buffett. As I write, they are number one and two on the *Forbes* list of the wealthiest people in the world. Yet they took totally different approaches to accumulating their wealth.

Bill Gates achieved his wealth by producing products and doing an incredibly good job of marketing them. Warren Buffett created his wealth through investments. He saved money, invested it very wisely, and earned huge returns. He generated capital from others and invested that money, too. While Bill Gates became rich through producing products, Warren Buffett became wealthy through providing capital so that companies could produce products.

Though these are totally different approaches to making money, they are two good ways to become financially independent. Within these two broad areas, there are many different approaches to take. If we want to take the Bill Gates approach, there are many industries we can go into. There are many skills we can employ. We can specialize in design, production, outsourcing, selling, marketing, and so on. If we take the Warren Buffett approach, we can invest in securities, real estate, start-up companies, and such. There is no shortage of ways to achieve a goal of financial independence if we will grow and persevere.

How do we know if we are persevering or just being stubborn? Remember the first key to success: Judge the seed by the harvest. If I want to be financially independent, I look to see where I am. If I am not closer to financial independence than I was a few years ago, then I am not being persistent. If I keep doing what I have always done even though it isn't getting me what I want, then I am being stubborn.

I may decide at twenty that I want to be financially independent. So I develop a plan. I decide to get a good education, find a good job, and work hard. That's the plan. In fact, it is a good plan. If I do those things, but at thirty I am no closer to financial independence that I was at twenty, I need to re-evaluate my plans. If I am nearing forty and I haven't made significant progress, I need to do some serious thinking.

The goal of financial independence is still a good one. But the plan to achieve it is lacking. I may need to add something to the good job and hard work part of the plan. I may need an investment strategy. I may need to find a business I can build part time. I don't necessarily need to quit the job. And getting a good education wasn't a bad idea. However, if the road I'm on isn't taking me where I want to go, I better look for an exit. I can't keep driving down the same road and hope it will take me somewhere it's not going.

This applies to all of life. Are my current health practices giving me the energy and vitality I desire? If not and if I don't change, I am being stubborn. I need to develop persistence.

How about my relationships? Are they what I want them to be? If not, then I shouldn't be stubborn and keep doing what I am doing. I should be persistent. I should set a goal of building better relationships and then start seeking out different ways to build the relationships I want.

Perseverance is always a virtue. Stubbornness is always a vice. So why are we stubborn more than we are persistent? Because perseverance is difficult.

KEY IDEA

Worrying is useless. Most of the things we worry about never happen. The things that really challenge us are things we never even see coming.

PERSEVERANCE IS DIFFICULT

I believe the best opening paragraph of any book in the whole field of personal development literature comes from Scott Peck's *The Road Less Traveled*. The very first sentence of the book simply reads, "Life is difficult." Peck then goes on to explain that once we understand and accept that life is difficult, life becomes a lot less difficult. We make life a lot more difficult by expecting it to be easy. When difficulties come our way, we are totally taken by surprise. We are not prepared to deal with the difficulties. The person who understands that problems will arise simply accepts them as part of life and deals with them. This makes life a lot easier.

Let me give you a slightly modified version of what Peck said. Perseverance is difficult. Once we understand that and accept that perseverance is difficult, it becomes a lot easier to persevere. If we think that we can persist in achieving anything significant without difficulties, we are in for a big surprise. The very nature of success is that it only comes after we have persevered. The very nature of perseverance is that we persevere through difficulties.

When we set a goal, we should resign ourselves to the fact that there will be difficulties. We shouldn't worry about them. In fact, worrying about them is totally useless. Most of the things we worry about will never occur. The things that will really hit us hard will be things we never expected. We can be certain that difficulties will come our way, but we can't worry too much about what they will be.

There are a few challenges we can count on. In discussing the previous key to success, we talked about fear. We said that our fears can keep us from taking action. I find that there are two main fears people have that keep them from trying something new. They are the fear that they will fail and the fear that they will be criticized.

I can state with absolute certainty that two things will happen to those of us who step out and take action. We will fail and we will be criticized. The two things we fear most will happen. There is no way around it. We shouldn't try to find the route to success that bypasses fear and failure. There isn't one. We must learn how to navigate through fear and failure to achieve our goals anyway.

The key to success isn't to eliminate the things we fear. It is to persevere through them. Successful people accept that they will be criticized and that they will fail. It's not fun being criticized and it hurts to fail. However, these are simply things we must learn to handle if we want to master perseverance. So let's discuss each of these individually.

FAILURE

The road to success is paved with failure. If we aren't failing, it doesn't mean we are on the road to success. It means we've never left the garage. It's hard for us to get somewhere while avoiding the very road that will get us there.

To succeed, we must persevere through failure. There are three great myths about failure. As long as we hold on to these myths, we will never succeed. Let's see what those three great myths are.

KEY IDEA

The road to success is paved with failure. If we aren't failing, it doesn't mean we are on the road to success. It means we haven't left the garage.

Myth 1: Successful People Don't Fail

The biggest myth people have about failure is that successful people don't experience it. We tend to think that success is the absence of failure. If that's so, then I am a better golfer than Tiger Woods.

If you don't believe me, listen to this incredible record. In the last three years, I've lost fewer tournaments than Tiger Woods. I've missed fewer putts than Tiger Woods. I've bogied fewer holes than Tiger Woods. In fact, in every dimension of the game of golf, I've made fewer mistakes than Tiger Woods. Do you know how I've developed such an incredible record? I haven't picked up a golf club in the past three years.

Now, obviously not playing the game doesn't make me better than someone who does. But that's the exact type of thinking that is involved when we believe that success is the absence of failure. Study any successful person and you will find that their lives were filled with failures.

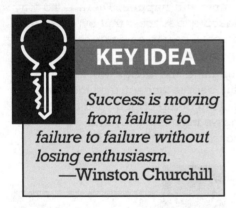

KEY IDEA

Success is moving from failure to failure to failure without losing enthusiasm.
—Winston Churchill

If it weren't for Winston Churchill, Hitler probably would have won. As much as anyone, Churchill is responsible for saving Europe from all falling under dictatorial rule. Not bad. I would call that pretty successful. Still, here was Churchill's view of success. He said that success is going from failure to failure to failure without losing enthusiasm.

Have you ever heard of a Honda? Do you know what a Honda was before it was a car? It was a motorcycle. What was a Honda before it was a motorcycle? It was a bicycle. What was a Honda before it was bicycle? It was a person. Mr. Honda. Soichiro Honda was the founder of Honda Motor Corporation which employs more than 100,000 people. His name has become a noun. Not bad for a person who said, "Success is 99% failure." He failed 99% of the time and created a multibillion-dollar international corporation.

Another business success was Thomas Watson. He took over a small company with just a handful of employees. He renamed it International Business Machines, or IBM as we know it. When he retired, IBM had 50,000 employees. Not bad. Someone once asked Watson how to increase the number of successes. His answer was to double your failure rate.

Study the life of Abraham Lincoln. It was rife with failure. Let me give you a brief synopsis. He failed. He failed. He failed. He failed. He failed. He failed. He failed. He failed. He was elected president. He saved the union. Lincoln failed a lot more than he succeeded, but he isn't remembered as a failure. There is a big monument in Washington, D.C. that pays tribute to him as a pretty big success.

The world of sports isn't any different. Babe Ruth is known as one of the best baseball players in history. Yet he struck out far more than anyone else during his playing days. Someone once asked Ruth what he thought about when he struck out. He said, "Hitting more home runs." Athletes have won/loss records. To find one with a zero in the loss column, we'd have to look for athletes with few wins in the win column. The more you play, the greater the odds you will experience failure.

We should be passionate about winning. We should be disappointed when we don't win. However, we must recognize the worst loss of them all is to not compete. Jim Rohn put it best when he said, "When the story of your life is written, let it show your wins, and let it show your losses. But don't let it show that you didn't play. How would you explain that?"

Myth 2: Smart People Don't Fail

We often think that we fail because we are stupid. "If I had just been smarter" we think, "this wouldn't have happened."

Smart people fail. Albert Einstein was pretty smart. Everyone would agree that he is one of the smartest people who ever lived. Everyone but Einstein, that is. One time, he said, "It's not that I am smarter than everyone else, it's just that I stick with the problem longer." Did you catch that? He didn't attribute his discovery to his brains but to his perseverance. He also said, "I think and I think for weeks and months at a time. Ninety-nine times I am wrong, and the hundredth time I am right."

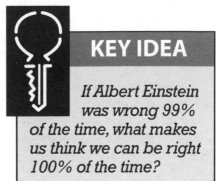

KEY IDEA

If Albert Einstein was wrong 99% of the time, what makes us think we can be right 100% of the time?

Now, if Albert Einstein was wrong 99% of the time, what makes us think that we can be right 100% of the time? We must never be afraid to make mistakes.

One of the smartest leaders I have ever seen in action is Colin Powell. Powell is smart enough to risk failing. When he was a commander in the Army, Colin Powell had a rule. He said that he would try to get enough information to have between a 40% and 70% chance of success. Less than 40% and he needed to gather more information. However, over 70% was usually just as bad. If you wait until you have more information beyond that point, your opportunity has passed you by. The smartest people in the world must live with being wrong some of the time.

KEY IDEA

We don't want to avoid making mistakes. We want to avoid making stupid mistakes.

Now, the number of allowable failures may vary from situation to situation based on the severity of the consequences. For example, I don't want the pilot of the plane I'm on to be satisfied with a 70% chance of landing the thing. I don't want my surgeon to have a 40% chance of getting it right. I don't want him to keep lopping off parts until he finally gets the right one. There are times when failure is devastating. However, we shouldn't flatter ourselves and think that what we do requires such brains that we can't fail.

Smart people take smart risks. Others take no risks or take stupid risks. A smart person looks at the good that could come from success, the harm that could come from failure, and the chances of each. If the upside potential justifies the downside risk, then they will take a chance. If they fail, that's okay. They made a smart mistake.

We don't want to avoid mistakes. We want to avoid *stupid* mistakes. For example, getting sloppy drunk, hopping in the car, and heading home would be a stupid mistake. Even if we made it home safely, we made a stupid decision. All we did was save cab fare. However, we risked killing ourselves or someone else, being arrested, losing our driver's license and insurance, destroying our car, and the like. These risks are real because drunk drivers do those things every day. To risk them just to save cab fare isn't the kind of risk a smart person would take.

Myth 3: Talented People Never Fail

Failure can make us feel so goofy. We think that the talented people of this world don't fail. If we were just more talented, we tell ourselves, we wouldn't fail. Nothing could be further from the truth.

One of the best basketball players of all time was Michael Jordan. Someone once asked him what made him so successful. Here's what he said.

"I've lost almost three hundred games. I've missed over nine thousand shots. Twenty-six times when the game was on the line, I took the shot and missed. That's why I've been so successful."

Jordan understood success. He understood that talented people fail. In fact, because of the position they put themselves in, they fail at a much bigger level. When they fail, more is at stake and more people notice.

We will never fully utilize our talents without failing over and over again. Sure, Michael Jordan had incredible abilities. However, he got the most out of those abilities because he wasn't afraid to fail. He once said, "I can accept failing. Everyone fails at something. I can't accept not trying."

The true greatness of Michael Jordan wasn't seen on the basketball court but on the baseball field. Yes, I know that he never did very well there. That is what showed his greatness. He was willing to leave his position as the dominant player

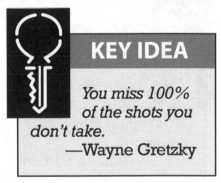

KEY IDEA

You miss 100% of the shots you don't take.
—Wayne Gretzky

in all of basketball and take on a different challenge. People miss the point when they say he failed. The point was that he risked failure.

Who is the greatest athlete of my generation? I am not even a hockey fan and my vote goes to Wayne Gretzky. Everybody knows what a great scorer he was. Before Gretzky, the single-season points record was 152. His record was 215. That's an increase of over 40%. One year, Gretzky could've stopped playing on January 7, almost three months before the end of the season, and still won the scoring title.

He didn't just hog the puck so he could score. His assist record was even more impressive than his scoring. The eight greatest assist seasons in NHL history all belong to Gretzky, not to mention the tenth, eleventh, and twelfth spots, too. He broke Gordie Howe's all-time assist record in 1,086 fewer games, or thirteen fewer seasons, than it took Howe to set it.

How did he accomplish so much? It certainly wasn't by being afraid to try. He once said, "You miss 100% of the shots you don't take." Even if you're the Great One, you will still miss some of the shots you take and all of the ones you don't take.

DEALING WITH FAILURE

I had a student who flunked her first exam. She told me that all hope was gone. She flunked the test, so she would probably flunk the class. If she couldn't pass this class, she would probably never graduate. Since there were no opportunities unless you have a college degree, what would she do? I thought she was about to crawl to the top of the Business School building and jump.

> **KEY IDEA**
>
> *Failure is just the opportunity to begin again more intelligently.*
> —Thomas Edison

Our problem isn't that we fail. Our problem is how we deal with failure. I encouraged this student to calm down and analyze her failure. There was a reason she didn't do well on the exam. I told her to figure out what she did wrong, make adjustments, and do better on the next exam. She did so, and she actually made a good grade in the class.

Ken Blanchard said that successful people are the ones who are fascinated with what doesn't work. When we analyze our failures, we are using them as stepping stones to eventual victories.

Here's why. We are in a better position to achieve our goals after trying and failing than we were before we ever even tried. Thomas Edison said, "Failure is just the opportunity to begin again more intelligently." If we analyze our failures, learn from them, adjust, and keep on going, then our failures can be good for us. I know I've personally learned a lot more from one failure than all my successes combined.

CRITICISM

The loudest sounds we will hear on our success journey are the cries of the critics. It's not that critics are the only ones watching. They are just the ones with the biggest mouths.

There are a few people who don't have a life, so they spend theirs criticizing everyone who does. These people are not more than 10% of any group. However, they are the vocal minority, so it appears they speak for everyone.

The critics are always talking about people who are doing things with their lives. The only way to shut a critic up is to say nothing, do nothing, and be nothing. Actually, that won't shut them up, either. They will just find someone else to talk about.

My wife and I have a philosophy about critics. We know they are going to talk about someone. It might as well be us. Let's give them something to talk about. When we see something that needs to be done, we do it. When the critic says it can't be done, we make sure it can. In our lives, critics don't matter. If they had a life, they wouldn't have time to sit around criticizing ours.

Teddy Roosevelt said it best:

"It is not the critic who counts. Not the man who points out how the strong man stumbled or where the doer of deeds could have done better. The credit belongs to the man who is actually in the arena, whose face is marred by dust and sweat and blood; who strives valiantly; who errs and comes short again and again because there is no effort without errors and shortcomings; who knows the great enthusiasms, the great devotions; who spends himself in a worthy cause. Who, at the best, knows in the end the triumph of high achievement, and who at the worst, at least fails while daring greatly, so that his place shall never be with those timid souls who know neither victory nor defeat."

Sure, the critic may be able to point out the faults in our actions. But, as Roosevelt said, all actions have faults. It is better to have actions, as flawed as they may be, than to sit there and know neither victory nor defeat.

Never take a critic seriously. Remember, though, that not everyone who criticizes us is a critic. Sometimes they just don't see what we see. One time, I heard a speaker explain it this way. The guy lived on the inland waterway down at the gulf. All the people in his neighborhood had personal docks. One day, he walked out his back door with his dog. He saw a heron sitting on their dock.

KEY IDEA

On our success journey, the loudest sounds we will hear will be the cries of the critics.

The dog took off running. He wanted that bird. However, the heron wasn't going to sit there and let the dog gobble him up. As soon as the dog got half way down the dock, the heron gently flew over to the neighbor's dock. The dog stopped, turned around, and went next door as fast as he could. The heron simply flew from dock to dock until the dog collapsed in total exhaustion.

The speaker thought it was so funny to see the dog running around trying to catch this bird. Then he asked the audience a question. "What would I have thought if I didn't see the bird?" What if all he saw was his dog running around as fast as he could from dock to dock barking and stirring up a bunch of sand? The speaker said he wouldn't have thought that was funny. He would have thought something was wrong with the dog.

Most of the time, when we are pursuing our purpose in life, people can't see what we're doing. We have a vision of what we want or where we want to be. Our vision is in our mind. We may try to explain it to people, but most can't see it. If they could see our vision, they would applaud us for what we are doing. Instead, all they see is us running around and they think we're crazy. Often, when we're being criticized, there is nothing wrong with us and there is nothing wrong with the person criticizing us. They just don't see what we see.

IF WE PERSIST

One day, if we persevere, we will have our victory. We will have faced our fears and conquered them along the way. There will have been failures, but they won't matter. We don't have to succeed the first time we try. We only have to succeed the last time we try.

Along the way, there will be critics. They don't matter, either. When we win, they will be off to find some other worthy soul to criticize.

Everyone else will stand up and cheer. We probably shouldn't take their cheers too seriously. What we should take seriously is that we didn't quit doing what we were meant to do.

Of course, that assumes we know what we should be doing. How do we know what we should persist at? Well, that's the sixth key to all success.

KEY IDEA

Most of the time, when we are pursuing our purpose in life, people can't see what we're chasing. If they could, they would applaud us.

KEY 6

When you're average, you're just as close
to the bottom as you are the top.
—Anonymous

PURPOSE: BE UNIQUE, NOT AVERAGE

As we are growing up, our biggest desire is to fit in. The last thing we want to do is stick out in a crowd. So we become very conscious of those things that make us unique. We don't want to be different. We just want to be normal.

One big problem with being normal. *Normal means average.* If we never do anything different from what everyone else is doing, then we will never have anything more than what everyone else has. The only way to achieve more than the average person is to quit being average. Be unique.

I tell my students that normal means average. Then I ask them, "What part of average do you want?" I start by asking them if they want an average marriage.

Do you know what the average marriage in America is? Divorce. Over half the marriages in the U.S. end in divorce. What about the ones who don't? Do you think they are filled with love, hugs, and kisses all the time? Being gracious, I would say that half of them aren't too good. That means that if you do what everyone else does when it comes to marriage, you have less than a 25% chance of having a good one. I certainly don't want an average marriage.

What about an average job? I give my students the statistics of the average household income in our country. I then ask my materialistic business students how many of them want to spend their lives living on that much money. They all want more. I tell them if they accept being average, they won't earn any more than the average worker.

How about being an average parent? The president of my university once told me that only 30% of the students who graduate from high school in our region qualify for admission to our school. Almost half

KEY IDEA

Normal means average. Fitting in means being average. What part of average do we want? It is only our uniqueness that can propel us beyond mediocrity.

of those students won't qualify to get into our College of Business. So, if you want your kid to have the option of getting a good education, you had better not be an average parent.

On and on I could go. The normal life is an average life. Fitting in means being average. Since average isn't that great, we should stop trying to fit in. We were made to be unique, not average. We must embrace our uniqueness. That is what can propel us beyond mediocrity to a life of greatness. It will be the thing that helps us fulfill our unique purpose in life.

MAKING A DIFFERENCE

Our job in life isn't to blend into the scenery. Our job is to find our unique purpose in life and fulfill it. That means we find a place where we can make an impact. Then we do what we can do to make a difference in someone else's life.

As a man walked down the beach, all he could see were starfishes everywhere. The tide had washed thousands upon thousands of them ashore. They were dying in the hot sun. Every few steps, the man would bend down, pick up a starfish, and throw it back into the ocean.

"What are you doing?" someone on the beach asked. "The beach is littered with dying starfish. You can't possibly make a difference."

The man reached down, picked up another starfish, tossed it into the water and said, "I just made a difference to that one."

We are all walking down the same beach. Some people are making a difference, some are not. There are those who could step on a starfish and never notice. They aren't making a difference because they can't see the needs that are around them on every side. There are those who see the enormity of the needs around them and are overwhelmed. They can't do everything, so they don't do anything. Then there are the successful ones. They are the people who make a difference where they can.

A PURPOSE WORTH FULFILLING

It isn't hard to find a purpose worthy of our lives. We only need to open our eyes.

People are hurting. Children are starving. There are those who don't know how to read and write. Freedom must be defended. The environment must be protected. Society is in the midst of a moral decline. Living standards are increasing, and people are looking for better ways to enjoy their affluence. Technology is advancing. We need things that will make us smile. We also need things that will make us think and reflect. There is money to be made, enjoyed, spent, and given away. Every day, lives are destroyed by addictions to alcohol and drugs. Hospitals must be staffed so that lives can be saved

KEY IDEA

If we but look around, we can find a purpose in life beyond mastering the TV remote.

and babies can be born. Children must be taught to read and write and care. We need hope for the hopeless and friends for the friendless. There are families who are being crushed under the weight of financial disaster. Others are looking for ways to enjoy more time together. Not all truths have been discovered. There are highways and cities to be built. Food must be grown and harvested or we all will perish. There is still music to be made and poetry to be written. Who will sing it? Who will read it?

On and on we could go about both the problems we face and the possibilities that lie before us. Certainly, if we but look around us, we can find something to do beyond mastering the TV remote. The big challenge shouldn't be in finding something to do. The big challenge should be to zero in on what we should be doing. We can make a difference. How do we decide what difference we should make?

FINDING OUR PURPOSE

Barbara Sher wrote a book titled *I Could Do Anything If I Only Knew What It Was*. That book is quite popular among my students, most likely due to the title. As they approach graduation, they know they should do something significant with their lives, yet many of them don't know what that something is.

It isn't like an algebra problem where, if we just apply the right formula, the right answer will pop up. There is no magic formula for finding out what we should do with our life. However, there are a few keys that will help us find our purpose in life. They are:

- Try a Bunch of Stuff
- Ask a Bunch of Questions
- Follow Our Heart
- Build on Our Strengths
- Go with What We Know

Let's look at each of these individually.

TRY A BUNCH OF STUFF

You can't steer a parked car. Even if my car is heading in the wrong direction, I must get it moving before I can get it heading in the right direction. The most basic principle of finding our purpose in life is to try stuff.

How can we ever know if we like something different if we never try anything different? Through trying stuff, we discover some very important things. We find out what our talents are. We identify things we like doing and things we don't like doing. We discover ways we can make an impact and ways that our efforts count for nothing. However, we won't discover any of those things until we step out and try.

Tom Peters said:

"Life is pretty simple. You do some stuff. Most of it fails. Some works. You do more of what works. If it works big, others quickly copy it. Then you do something else. The trick is doing something else."

When we try something, it is no disgrace to give it up if we discover it isn't for us. That doesn't mean we're quitters. It simply means we are in the looking stage. We must be careful, though, not to quit too fast. We must stick with something long enough to get through the initial frustration and embarrassment that always comes with trying something new.

In life, we are always presented with opportunities to try new things. I moved to a new town when I was in eighth grade. Where I had lived before didn't have youth football, and in my new town, boys started playing organized football in the third grade. Every kid in the school knew if he wanted to play football because they had already played on a team. But I didn't know if I would like it or not. I had never tried it.

So what did I do? Well, I could have gone around asking all the kids in the class if I should go out for the team. What answer would I have gotten? Well, that would depend on who I asked. If I asked the members of the Chess Club, they would probably say no. If I asked the members of the football team, they would probably say yes. Which answer would be right? They wouldn't be giving me answers that are right for me. They would be giving me answers that were right for them. The only way I could know if football was right for me was to try out myself. That is what I did. I discovered I didn't like football. I stayed with the team through the whole season, and I didn't like any of it. So I never played organized football again.

KEY IDEA

How can we know if we would like something different if we never try anything different?

Then came basketball season. Would I like it? How could I tell? I tried out for the basketball team. I didn't particularly like it at the start, but by the end of the season, I was really enjoying it. I found something I enjoyed for many years of my life.

That's exactly how we find out what we should do with our lives. We try something. We stick with it long enough to get a good feel for what it is like. Then we either commit to mastering it or we find something else to try. Never quit too early. Never be afraid to try something new.

As we are trying, we must always remember that we are seeking. Our goal is not to jump from one thing to another. Our goal is to find something and stick with it to completion. The reward isn't for trying something. The reward is for finding something we want to do and then, through commitment, mastering it.

ASK A BUNCH OF QUESTIONS

The New Testament says, "Ask and it shall be given unto you, seek and you shall find, knock and the door shall be open unto you." If that's true, receiving is reserved for those who ask, finding is reserved for those who seek, and open doors are reserved for those who knock. We can't expect to find and receive if we never seek and ask. We can't expect open doors if we never knock.

Seek answers. Ask questions. What questions? Let me give you two good questions for starters.

What Do I Want?

I have heard a gazillion people say they just don't know what they want to do. "I keep asking myself, 'What do I want to do?' and I can't find the answer." They aren't finding the right answer because they aren't asking the right question. Don't ask, "What do I want to do?" Ask, "What do I want?" Then do what it takes to get it.

One time, I was asked to teach a consumer research seminar in Europe. I didn't really want to do it. My schedule was already packed. It was a three-day seminar and I had a five-day window to work with. I would have to fly over there, speak for three days, immediately board a plane and fly right back. I set my fees very high hoping I would price myself out of the market. To my amazement, they accepted my offer.

KEY IDEA

Don't ask, "What do I want to do?" Ask, "What do I want?" Then do what it takes to get it.

I told a friend of mine who is an economist that I really didn't want to go. I was making the trip just for the money. I will never forget what he said. "That's why they're paying you. People pay us to do the things we don't want to do. If it were something you wanted to do, they probably wouldn't have to pay you."

Teenagers like to be entertained, and they don't like to carry groceries around. That is why teenagers get paid to bag groceries at the supermarket and why they, in turn, pay money to get into the movies.

I heard a basketball star explain it this way. Someone said that he was so lucky because he got paid to play basketball. He quickly responded that he did not get paid to play basketball. He would play basketball for free. He would even pay people to let him play basketball. If they weren't paying him, he would still play basketball as much as he could.

What he was getting paid for was practicing for hours on end. He wouldn't do that if he weren't getting paid. He was getting paid to leave his family, sometimes for weeks at a time, to play road games. He wouldn't do that if he weren't getting paid. He was getting paid for attending press conferences, playing when he was hurt and totally exhausted, and all kinds of other stuff he wouldn't do if he weren't getting paid.

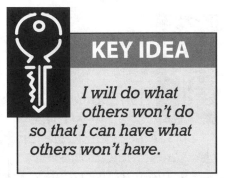

KEY IDEA

I will do what others won't do so that I can have what others won't have.

The team had to pay him a lot of money to get him to continue doing a whole lot of stuff he didn't like doing. If he weren't getting paid, he would just buy a membership at the gym, play basketball when he felt like it, and skip all the other stuff he didn't like doing.

A powerful statement to live our lives by is this: "I will do what others won't do so that I can have what others can't have." We must decide what we want from life and then do whatever we need to do to get it. If we always do what we want to do, then we will never get to do what we *really* want to do. However, if we do what we don't want to do often enough and get paid for it, then one day we will get to do exactly what we want to do.

I am not advocating that we spend our lives working in a field we hate. Quite the opposite. I love my job, but I didn't love all the things I had to do to get it. I did a lot of stuff I didn't want to do so I could do the thing I really wanted to do. Often, people will tell me that they would love to teach at a university. I tell them with excitement that being a professor is the greatest job on the planet. Then I tell them that, if they want to teach at that level, they need to earn a doctorate. Colleges hire instructors who don't have Ph.D.'s, but around a university, you will always be a second-class citizen if you don't have a doctoral degree.

"I don't know if I want to do that," they often say.

"Of course, you don't," I exclaim. "Nobody in their right mind wants to go through the sacrifices and pain of a Ph.D. program. Still, if you want to really enjoy the life of a college professor, that is the price you have to pay. You have to do what you don't want to do if you ever want to do what you really want to do."

What Is the Value?

Many people spend their lives asking, "What is the price?" when they should be asking, "What is the value?" To get higher quality, we must pay a higher price. If we spend our lives obsessed with price, we will never have quality. Paying more will not necessarily get us better quality. However, we can never get higher quality without paying more. Not everything that costs more is better, but everything that is better costs more.

> **KEY IDEA**
>
> *We shouldn't find the lowest price and settle with whatever value it may give. We should find the value we want and then pay whatever price is required.*

If we want a quality life, then we need to be quality seekers and not bargain hunters. If we walk through life always looking for the lowest price, then we will be filling our lives with cheap stuff. If we want a cheap life, always look to pay the lowest price possible. If we want a quality life, we must quit looking at the price and start looking at the value.

We mustn't set goals because they are easy to achieve. If we do, we won't have much when we achieve them. We should set goals that will add value to our life. Then, when we achieve them, we will have something valuable. We shouldn't find the lowest price and settle with whatever value it may give. We should find the value we want and then pay whatever price is required.

Follow Our Heart

A famous filmmaker with a long history of failed relationships once quipped that he had a hard time getting his head and heart to agree. "In fact," he said, "they are seldom even on speaking terms." I am sure we've all experienced the frustration of trying to get our mind and our emotions onto the same page. When we can't get our heart and head together, which one should we listen to? It depends.

If we're thinking of getting married, we should listen to both our heart and our head. If they're not in agreement, then we should probably stay single.

When the alarm clock goes off on a cold winter morning, we should ignore both our emotions and our intellect. Instead, we should listen to the commitment we made the night before when we set it. Our heart will beg us to stay in bed, and it will enlist our head to come up with good reasons to do so.

When we've set a goal, we should use our heads and not our hearts to figure out the best way to achieve it. Our emotions are terrible at making good, solid, logical, objective decisions.

There is one time, however, when we must listen to our heart and not our head. That is when we are deciding on our purpose in life. Here, we should follow our heart and not our head. Here's why. In order to achieve anything great in life, we will have to overcome incredible obstacles. There will

KEY IDEA

Any time we do something big, it is difficult. At some point, it stops making sense. At that point, if we are following our head and not our heart, we will quit.

come a time when our minds will say, "This doesn't make sense any more." At that time, if our heart isn't engaged, we will quit. We will stop and move on to something that is easier.

That's why I encourage my students to follow the career path that interests them, not their parents. Mom and Dad do a great job of figuring out the logical thing Junior should do with his life. Often, it makes great sense … except Junior isn't interested. If he goes along with it, Mom and Dad will be delighted, but Junior will be miserable. They don't feel his emotions.

I tell them to listen to Mom and Dad's advice. Take their wisdom and experience into consideration. But in the end, make your own choice. It won't be Mom and Dad who will have to show up at your desk at 8:00 a.m. They won't be the ones who have to do your job. You will be the one who will have to endure the endless hours of doing something you hate. Find something that grabs your heart. If you don't find it, keep looking. Don't let someone else tell you what to love. It doesn't work that way. You are the only one who can feel the passion. Follow your passion.

That doesn't necessarily mean that our passion has to be our vocation. A good friend of mine is one of the top young life insurance salespersons in the country. We were having lunch the other day. He told me he enjoyed selling life insurance, but his real passion is working with children. He wasn't sure if he should keep doing what he is good at or if he should quit and start doing what he really loves.

I suggested that he throw everything he has into his career for a few years. With his skills, he could build up his business to the point he could work just a few hours a week and still bring in a good income. Then he could do whatever he wanted to do with kids.

If, on the other hand, he quit selling insurance and started working with kids, he would have to think about money when he decided which kids to work with. He would have to find a job that paid. Not only that, his salary would be a financial drain on the children's program he would be working with. If he built his financial independence, he could choose whatever children's program he wanted to work with, and his presence would not drain its resources.

Our passion need not be our vocation. Our vocation may simply be something we are good at which gives us the resources we need to pursue our real love in life.

Build upon Our Strengths

When Jack Welch took over as CEO of General Electric in 1981, the company was doing well, but it had over 350 business units. Welch felt that no company could manage that many units effectively. He had to decide which units to divest and which units to grow. He made the decision based on business strength. If a business unit couldn't be number one or two in the world marketplace, Welch got rid of it.

That left a mere fourteen business units. However, GE was uniquely positioned in each of those fourteen areas to be a world-class competitor. With 350 business units, GE was doing well. When it moved to fourteen business units, GE increased its market capitalization twenty-fold in less than twenty years and became the most valuable company on the planet. GE focused on their strengths and the payoff was phenomenal.

We all have something that makes us unique. We may have a unique talent. We may own something special or have certain experiences. We may have a driving passion that pushes us on when others stand still. We are uniquely positioned in life to accomplish something. We must not be afraid to take what makes us unique and do something unique with it.

I have two older brothers—Ed and Eb. (I am glad my parents changed the pattern of naming kids or I would be Egg.) Ed is a supervisor for a large mass transit authority. He has hundreds of people under his authority. Eb is a lawyer and a politician. I have joked that we each have the perfect jobs. Ed loves to tell people what to do, so he became a supervisor. Eb loves to argue, so he became a lawyer and a politician. I love to talk, so I became a professor.

KEY IDEA

We must not be afraid to take what makes us unique and do something unique with it.

Each of us is so unique and each is capable of accomplishing something great by taking advantage of what we are good at. I see the same things in my four children. I have one child who loves to learn. We call him the walking encyclopedia. Another child is very sensitive, with an artistic streak in her. I have a son who thinks night and day about making money. My younger daughter is so energetic we sometimes call her "the rocket." She is also very people oriented, with strong interpersonal skills. One of the exciting things about being a parent is watching our kids grow up, wondering how each will use their unique personalities to fill their own place in this world.

GO WITH WHAT WE KNOW

Life is short. We can't wait until we have all the answers before we step out. As a highly successful Hollywood executive once said, "I am always questioning my choices. My mother died in her late thirties, so I am painfully aware of the fact that life doesn't guarantee us a second half." Even if life does give us both halves, it's still short.

Michael Landon was one of the most handsome, vibrant, healthy looking stars Hollywood ever produced. Yet he died of cancer in his mid fifties. As he was facing death, here is what he said:

> "Somebody should tell us, right at the start of our lives, that we are dying. Then we might live life to the limit, every minute of every day. 'Do it!' I say. Whatever you want to do, do it now! There are only so many tomorrows."

We can't afford to wait until we know all the details of what we will do for the rest of our lives before we get started. Discovery is progressive.

Our purpose will be progressively revealed to us as we go through life acting on what we know.

On a university campus, few entering freshmen show up knowing what they want to do with their lives. In fact, most graduating seniors still aren't too sure. Most college students change their minds along the way. The majority of college graduates don't spend their careers in the fields for which they were trained. Does that mean that most college students are wasting their time? Should they wait until they know exactly what they want to do before they even go to college? Absolutely not.

KEY IDEA

We can't wait for all the lights on our route to be green before we leave the house.

Students may not know exactly what they'll be doing with their lives, but they do know they have more options with a college degree. There is an extremely good chance that their first choice for a career will require a college degree. By starting college, they can head off in a general direction of where they want to be. The details will work themselves out along the way.

The more we act on what we do know, the more our life's purpose will be revealed. The key is to do what we can with what we know while seeking to discover more. We can't wait for all the lights to be green before we leave the house.

NOT JUST ANOTHER PRETTY FACE

When I think of achieving great things through being unique, W. Mitchell comes to mind. He wrote the book appropriately titled *The Man Who Would Not Be Defeated*. As a young man, the motorcycle he was driving collided with a truck which had run a stop sign. When it's truck versus motorcycle, truck wins. If all his broken bones weren't bad enough, the gas tank on his motorcycle exploded and covered his body with flaming fuel. His face was badly scarred from the burns.

After a two-year medical recovery, he went on with his life. Then, some years later, the airplane he was flying crashed. When it's airplane versus ground, ground wins. This time he lost the use of both his legs.

While he was in therapy learning to deal with this life-changing experience, he met a despondent athlete who had also lost the use of his legs in an accident. Here's what Mitchell told him. "Before my accident, I could do ten thousand things. Now, I can do nine thousand things. If I only do a few of those things, I can have a great life and impact a lot of people."

Mitchell has done just that. He ventured into politics, becoming the mayor of Crested Butte, Colorado. He almost won a congressional seat running on the slogan "I Won't Be Just Another Pretty Face in Congress." He ventured into business, starting a successful company that put thousands of people to work. He ventured into television, making appearances in the United States and abroad. He developed a successful speaking career, receiving the CAPE award, which is the highest award given by the National Speakers Association. He earned his master's degree from the University of Colorado. Now, he has offices in Colorado and Australia and lives in California and Hawaii. Mitchell's favorite saying is "It's not what happens to you but what you do with it that matters."

It's hard to look at someone like W. Mitchell and not believe that we can make a difference in this world. How did he accomplish such incredible things? He didn't spend much time worrying about what he couldn't do. He saw what he could do. He made a difference where he was. He tried some things. Some worked. Some did not. He pursued a quality life and not a life of ease. He built on his strengths, even though he had some very notable weaknesses. He asked questions and he followed his passions. He was truly unique. That's what made him special.

You are unique, also. Tap into your uniqueness and discover your purpose, and you'll defeat "the enemy called average."

KEY 7

The man who dies rich dies disgraced.
—Andrew Carnegie

SACRIFICE: SEEK WEALTH, NOT RICHES

Andrew Carnegie had a couple of nephews who were attending Yale University. This was over a hundred years ago, so communication wasn't instantaneous, as it is today. U.S. mail was about the best they could do to stay in touch.

Unfortunately for Carnegie's sister, the boys didn't even use that. They must have been so caught up in the college life that they never wrote home. Their mother tried everything to get her sons to write. She begged, she pleaded, she tried putting them on a guilt trip. She just wanted to hear something from her sons. Anything would do.

Carnegie offered a wager to anyone who would take it. "I'll bet anyone $100 I can get the boys to write me a letter, and I won't even ask them to do so." A friend couldn't resist the offer and the bet was on.

Carnegie grabbed a piece of paper and a pen. He wrote the boys a short letter. This is all it said:

"I was just thinking about you and I knew how college kids can always use a little extra money. So, I am enclosing five dollars for you to spend however you want."

That was back when five dollars would go a long way for a college student. Carnegie sealed the letter and dropped it in the mail—only he didn't include the money.

As quick as the postal service could make it to New Haven and back, Carnegie had a letter from his nephews. "Dear Uncle Andy, we really appreciate your kindness, but ...." Carnegie won his bet.

USING HIS WEALTH TO MAKE A DIFFERENCE

Most of us spend our lives thinking that if we had a lot of money, we would know what to do with it. Andrew Carnegie actually did know how to use his wealth.

Proof of his philanthropy is scattered all over the country.

You can walk around Carnegie Mellon University. Visit Carnegie Hall. Check out a book from one of the 2,811 free libraries Carnegie built. Visit the website of the Carnegie Foundation, and see all the incredible contributions it is making to education. Check out the Carnegie Endowment for International Peace, and see what's happening there. Almost a century after he died, the one-time penniless immigrant who went on to found U.S. Steel is still making a difference in this world.

KEY IDEA

The bigger your gun, the higher you can aim.

Carnegie was smart enough to realize that the accumulation of money wasn't how he would change the world. A lot of people get rich, and all they leave behind is bunch of money for backbiting relatives to fight over.

On the other hand, Carnegie wasn't naive enough to think he could make much of a difference without creating some form of wealth. Money isn't the only way to make an impact. It is just the means that Carnegie chose. He made a huge impact on the world because he had a lot of money to do so. Carnegie had high aspirations in life. He also understood that the bigger the gun, the higher you can aim.

THE WEALTH OF A PERSON

KEY IDEA

Wealth is having what we need to achieve success.

Earlier, we defined success as having fun finding and fulfilling our purpose in life. We should all strive to be successful. In striving to be successful, we must also strive to be wealthy. Here's why.

Let's define wealth. Wealth is having what we need to achieve success. Put another way, we are wealthy if we have the resources we need to fulfill our purpose in life. What resources? That depends on the purpose. Our purpose might require us to have money. We might need to know the right people. We will probably need energy and good health. There will be things we need to know. Time is important, too. Wealth takes on many forms, but without some form of wealth, we can never do much with our lives.

KEY IDEA

If we don't have the wealth we need to fulfill our purpose, we might as well not have a purpose. It yields the same results.

In 1776, the year our country was founded, Scottish economist Adam Smith published the most important book ever written in the field of economics—*The Wealth of Nations*. Before Smith, people thought that the richest nations were the ones that had the most silver and gold. The more they had, the wealthier they were. All this focus on possessing wealth took everyone's attention away from what creates wealth—production. Smith argued that it was the ability to produce, not accumulate, that made a nation wealthy.

Today, no one seriously questions Smith's view of national wealth. However, this fact is often totally ignored when we think of personal wealth. We tend to think of people being wealthy because of what they have accumulated, not what they can do. Not so. Wealth should be seen in terms of what we can do, not what we have.

Getting wealthy should never be our primary goal in life. It should always be secondary. Wealth is an enabler. It enables us to pursue our primary goals, which are tied into our life's purpose.

That doesn't mean we can skip the wealth-creation process. If we never get what we need to fulfill our purpose, we might as well not have a purpose. It yields the same results. We can't think like the naive salesperson who says, "I have a great prospect. He really likes our product. He just doesn't have the money to pay for it." If a person can't pay for the product, he isn't a prospect. Even if we want to succeed, we won't if we don't have the resources.

WEALTH FORMS

If we are serious about fulfilling our purpose in life, we will be serious about acquiring whatever we need to achieve our purpose. Wealth enables us to do more with our lives. Wealth comes in five basic forms. Let's take a moment to look at each of these, starting with the most obvious—money and possessions.

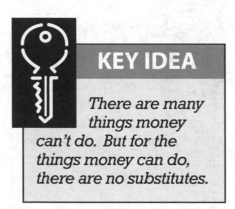

KEY IDEA

There are many things money can't do. But for the things money can do, there are no substitutes.

Money and Possessions

Most people could do a better job of fulfilling their purpose in life if they did a better job with their finances. Here's why. By itself, money is nothing but a bunch of pictures and numbers on paper. However, what those pictures and numbers enable us to do is quite significant.

"Money can't buy happiness," so the saying goes. That is absolutely true. Money can't buy happiness, but there are a lot more things happiness can't buy that money can.

Next time you go to the supermarket, fill up your cart with groceries. Then when the checker says, "That will be $183.29," take your warm, happy smile, and run it through their credit card machine. See if the checker keeps bagging your groceries. No, money won't buy happiness, but happiness won't put food on the table.

Try this. Go to your bank next time the mortgage payment comes due. Give them a big smile and say, "This month, I thought I would pay you with my wonderfully pleasant disposition." Then ask for a receipt. See what you get. No, money won't buy happiness, but happiness won't keep a roof over your head.

How about this one? Next time there is a famine, don't send money to the relief agency. Instead, send them a postcard telling them how happy you are. Have them pass it around the famine-ravaged country, so they will think pleasant thoughts to feed their empty stomachs. No, money can't buy happiness, but happiness won't feed starving kids.

Next time your child is sick or injured and needs a doctor, give this one a try. When the nurse asks you for your insurance policy, say this.

"I'm sorry, I don't have a health insurance policy. But I do have a policy around my house that we are happy all the time. Credit the doctor's fees on my happiness policy." Money doesn't buy happiness, but happiness won't get you a doctor's appointment.

Enroll for a class at your local university. When your bill arrives, go down to the Bursar's Office. Wait in line. Then, with the very best smile you can muster, say, "I don't have any money to pay my tuition, but I promise, I will be the absolute happiest person in every one of my classes." I know for certain that universities would rather have classrooms full of grumps with deep pockets than happy students who can't pay their tuition. Money can't buy happiness, but happiness won't pay for a good education.

Money can't make your kids love you, but it can make sure they stay in touch. The Beatles were right when they sang, "Money can't buy me love." However, when doing the dating thing, money certainly can increase your dating opportunities. Marrying for money is one of the stupidest things you can do. But trying to raise a family while being dead broke isn't a particularly good idea, either.

Here's the point. Money can't do most of the most important things in life. If all we have is money, we don't have much. But there are a few very important things only money can do. For the things money can do, there are no substitutes. Being controlled by money can be a huge problem. Being controlled by the lack of money isn't the solution. Money makes a terrible master, but it makes a wonderful servant.

It will take some money to fulfill our purpose in life. Exactly how much money will be determined by the purpose. We shouldn't necessarily aspire to be the richest person in our town, but we should aim at the level of financial wealth that will enable us to achieve our goals.

Health and Fitness

There is another great enabler in our life. It is our level of physical fitness. I am convinced that the biggest reason for underachievement in America is lack of vision. However, not far behind

> **KEY IDEA**
>
> *The biggest reason people don't achieve success is lack of vision. The second biggest reason is lack of energy.*

is the lack of energy that comes from a poor diet, inadequate exercise, not enough rest, and the inability to properly deal with stress. It takes energy to fulfill our purpose. We should not let inattention to our health diminish the impact we make in life.

We should hesitate to blame aging for our lack of energy. About ten years ago, I changed jobs. At the time, I was several pounds overweight, and I wasn't paying attention to any of the keys to good health. I attributed my declining energy to getting older. Fortunately, at my new job, I moved in right next to a colleague named Bill, who is fifteen years older than I am. Bill was full of energy. He was probably the most productive member of the faculty. I saw him work out at the gym, and he could do things few of our undergraduates could do.

Bill blew my age excuse right out of the water. For the next few months, I was constantly asking Bill what he did to stay in such good shape. I also began reading books on the subject. The more I incorporated good health practices into my life, the more energy I had. Eventually, all the aches, pains, and lack of energy that I had blamed on age disappeared. I discovered my problem wasn't my age. It could all be attributed to poor diet and lack of proper exercise.

Mind Power

Poor health can seriously limit our potential. However, good physical condition can only add so much to our lives. Sure, toning up the body is important. But tuning up the mind is even more important.

KEY IDEA

In the information age, it's not factories or land that makes us rich. It's mind power.

How much money can we make with physical labor? Even at your peak physical condition, you'd be lucky to earn a few thousand dollars a month as a laborer. Not that there's anything the matter with physical labor. Someone has to dig the ditches, repair the roads, and mow the city parks. However, the income potential of physical labor is quite limited. On the other hand, what kind of money can our minds generate? Bill Gates is worth tens of billions of dollars. I have seen Bill Gates. Trust me, he didn't make it with his body. It was his brains.

Our greatest potential for gains, both economic and noneconomic, comes from our ability to grow our minds, not our bodies. Yet, which ones do we always make sure we feed? If we miss one meal, the world is likely to hear about how hungry we are. If we miss two, our world begins to collapse. Three meals missed is martyrdom. Our bodies get all the food they need to survive—and then some.

Yet we can go day after day, week after week, month after month, year after year, and never feed our mind anything of substance to make it grow. Jim Rohn once said that many people feed their minds so little that they have rickets of the brain. A mind is a terrible thing to starve.

For most of human existence, we were in the Agricultural Age. Back then, the people with all the money and power were the ones who owned land. Everyone else was poor and worked for them. Then along came the Industrial Age. The people who got rich in the Industrial Age were the ones who owned the factories. If you wanted wealth in the industrial age, you had to own a factory.

Now we are in the Information Age. Who has the advantage now? It isn't the people with the land. It isn't the ones with the factories. It is the people with the best ideas and information. The better minds we have, the more we can survive and thrive in the Information Age. Influence goes to the ones with the mind power.

Relationships

"It's not what you know, but who you know, that counts." How many times have we heard someone say that? The statement is partly true. What counts in business and life is what you know AND who you know. It doesn't do a lot of good to know all the right people if everyone thinks you're ignorant. On the other hand, all the brilliance in the

KEY IDEA

The most successful people spend their lives bringing people together.

world is useless unless it can be somehow shared with the world. Hermits don't have much of an opportunity to profit from all their smarts.

I have noticed that the most successful people in any field are the ones who have figured out how to benefit the most people. Sometimes the real successful ones are nothing more than people brokers. They have a wide network of people they stay in contact with. They spend their lives accumulating favors by bringing people together.

Sam is a good accountant who is always looking for new clients. George owns an auto repair shop and needs a good accountant. A people broker brings Sam and George together. Then the people broker can ask Sam for an accounting favor or George for help with the car.

I am not saying we go around figuring out who can help us and then only help those people. It doesn't work that way. We never know who might be able to help us, so we should help as many people as we can whenever we can. We build as many bridges as we can because we never know which ones we may need to cross.

One time, my office was in a building that had just been renovated. We were all really proud with the way it looked. Our dean had worked particularly hard raising the funds and overseeing the project, so he was proudest of all.

Not long after this renovation, one of my colleagues let me have a table that had been in her office upstairs. It was small and light, so I just dragged it to my office, not knowing that one of the legs of the table was scratching the floor every step of the way. Two main hallways in the business building had huge scratches all the way down the hall. These scratches led straight to my office.

It didn't take the dean long to notice the scratches. He was kind, but I could tell it really bothered him. That night, I went up to the business building and spoke to Freddie, who was on the janitorial staff. "When were you planning on buffing these floors?"

"About three weeks from now," he answered.

I told Freddie my story. I didn't want the dean seeing this scratch for three weeks and thinking about me every time he did. I asked Freddie if he could do me a favor and move the buffing up any sooner. He said he would look into it. The next morning, the scratches were gone.

For years I had been cultivating my friendship with Freddie. I didn't do so because I ever thought I would need a favor from him. I built a bridge not thinking I would ever need to cross it. But one day, when I needed a quick favor, I was glad I did.

Presidential historians have noted that the White House staff have adored some presidents, while the staff could barely tolerate other commanders-in-chief. Most notable in the adored category were

Teddy Roosevelt and Ronald Reagan. Roosevelt would treat every gardener, maid, or kitchen worker at the White House as though they were members of one big family. It is said that, when he came back to visit after having been out of office a few years, one of the cooks said that there hadn't been a fun moment since he had left. Reagan was so loved by his staff that, when his helicopter landed, the staff would say, "Daddy's home."

How much time did it take for Reagan and Roosevelt to treat the White House staff with kindness and respect? Not much. Did it help their political careers? Probably not. But it did make the White House a more enjoyable place to live and work.

Presidents don't need to cancel Cabinet meetings to play touch football on the front lawn with the janitorial staff. Like all of us, presidents need to spend the majority of their time with the major people in their lives. However, investing a little extra effort with people around us is simply a good thing, and the right thing, to do. The more people we know, and the more people we help along the way, the more we will be able to get things done. That will certainly be a great source of wealth.

Time

Bill Gates was born in 1955. That was the height of the baby boom, when more baby boomers were born than in any other year. These baby boomers have been trading hours for something ever since. Gates has been trading much of his time for money—lots and lots of it. In financial terms, he has been the best trader of us all.

God didn't give Bill Gates twenty-eight hours a day and the rest of us twenty. He gave us all the same. Bill Gates just found a way to take those twenty-four hours and turn them into tens of billions of dollars.

Nothing we get is free. It all costs us at least one thing—time. We all have the same amount of time, twenty-four fresh hours, each and every day. We all trade those twenty-four hours for something. How far we go in life will be determined by how good we are as traders. Time is the biggest wealth factor of them all. We can recapture riches. And health. And relationships. But once we squander time, it is gone forever. Because time is so precious, it needs to be measured in how much we have AND how well we spend it.

CREATING WEALTH

So, those are the five wealth forms. We need to get the right amount of each. The trick is not to get more of everything. More isn't always better. Having more than we need is often just as bad as not having enough.

Early in my career, I didn't have many options. I would jump on every opportunity that came my way. That was okay when there weren't many opportunities coming my way. However, the more things I did, the more things I was asked to do. Then I reached a point in my early thirties where the opportunities available to me exceeded my capacity to do them all. Things were happening in my personal and my professional life, and I was squeezed to the point of total exhaustion. Not only that, I wasn't doing a particularly good job at anything.

Everything I was doing owned a chunk of me. I bought a large house on a huge plot of land. It took a chunk of me to keep it up. My wife and I had another child. Another chunk of me was gone. I became an officer in an international professional organization. Another chunk was gone. I started a company. Another chunk was gone. Another child was born. Another chunk was gone. I took over teaching a large class of six hundred students. Another chunk was gone. I committed to certain writing projects. Another chunk was gone. I took a Sunday school department at church. Another chunk was gone. Another child was born. Another chunk was gone. I accepted speaking invitations. Another chunk was gone. An opportunity came along to expand my business. Another chunk was gone. Eventually, I ran out of chunks.

I could not fulfill my purpose in life because I was doing too many things. My number one purpose in life, raising my family, was getting crowded out by things that really weren't that important to me. My other major purpose was to change lives through my teaching, speaking, and writing. That was getting crowded out, too. In order to increase my wealth, I had to start getting rid of things. By my late thirties, I was more interested in figuring out how to get stuff out of my life rather than get more stuff into it.

I was doing well financially. That wasn't my problem. I also had the right people in my life to do everything I wanted to do, and more. My mind was expanding, though there were some major holes in my thinking that needed to be addressed. My biggest problems were in time management and in physical conditioning.

If I were to have rated my life on the five forms of wealth, here is what it would have looked like.

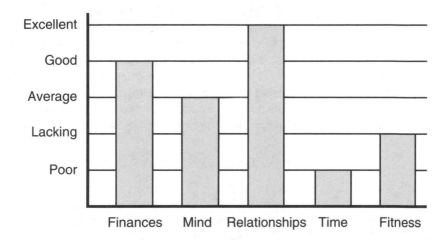

I was doing great in one area, poorly in another, and somewhere in between on the others. On average, I was doing okay. However, wealth doesn't work with averages. Wealth in one area cannot make up for poverty in another. There are five wealth forms, and we are never wealthier than our poorest wealth form.

I was doing a poor job of fulfilling my purpose in life because I was doing a poor job managing my time. For things to improve, I had to improve the way I was managing my time. To improve my finances at that point would have been futile. There was room for improvement, but gains there would not yield the great rewards that improving my time management skills would bring. Once I began to get my time under control, I had to go to work on my health. Only later would financial gains improve my life.

That's why some people are rich and miserable. They are doing excellent in the financial arena, but their relationships, time, and health may all be poor. That's also why many Hollywood stars live such messed-up lives. They have great fitness and lots of money. However, if they have no time and poor relationships, then they are poor. It takes all five to be wealthy. Seeking to max out one or two while ignoring the others is a sure formula for poverty.

TWO ROUTES TO WEALTH

A rating of excellent on a wealth form doesn't always come from getting more. Remember, being wealthy is having what we need to fulfill our purpose in life. If we add things to our life, and they aren't helping us fulfill our purpose, then we aren't getting wealthier. If they are distracting us from fulfilling our purpose, then we are actually getting poorer. Perhaps the following drawing can help us see what I mean.

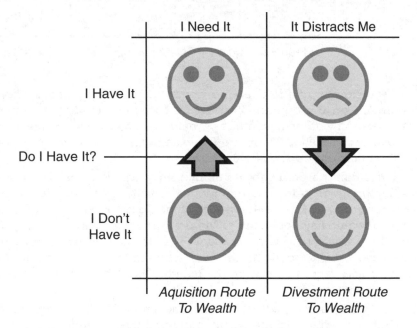

Do I Need It?/Does It Distract Me?

Wealth comes from having what we need and not being distracted by what we don't need. Poverty comes in two forms. There is a poverty of scarcity, which happens when we need what we don't have. This is what we typically think of when we think of poverty. However, there is also a poverty of bondage, when we are tied to things we don't need. Both poverties keep us from achieving success.

So how do we become wealthy? There are two routes we must take. If we need something but we don't have it, we get it. That is the acquisition route to wealth. When people think of getting wealthy, that is often the only route they see. There is also the divestment route. That's when we have stuff in our lives we don't need that keeps getting in our way, so we must get rid of it.

Getting more is not always the solution to our problems. One of the first things I had to do when I wanted to improve my quality of life was to start getting rid of some stuff. I changed jobs, sold my company, and moved to a smaller house on half the land. This allowed me to better manage my time and exercise regularly. Literally, within a few months, my quality of life skyrocketed. I massively improved my wealth in a very short time, not by acquiring more but by getting rid of what was distracting me from my real purpose in life.

SACRIFICE IS A VIRTUE

It's easy to judge the world by what you have. You look around. If you see someone who has more than you, they're greedy. If you see someone who doesn't have as much as you, they're lazy. The more you have, the more virtue you see in being wealthy. The less you have, the more virtue you see in being poor.

The virtuous life doesn't come from having a lot or a little. It comes from sacrificing what you do have to fulfill your purpose. Neither riches nor poverty is a virtue. The virtue is making a sacrifice to fulfill your purpose.

Albert Schweitzer was set for life. He was an incredibly talented musician whose skills were in high demand all over Europe. In addition to that, he had the best medical training and was a very influential physician. He was destined for a life of luxury and ease among the socially and economically elite of his day.

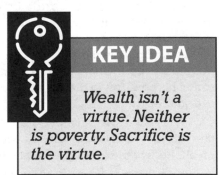

KEY IDEA

Wealth isn't a virtue. Neither is poverty. Sacrifice is the virtue.

But he felt a calling to serve as a medical missionary to the less fortunate in Africa. So he left the comfort and wealth of his home to go live out the rest of his life serving people who couldn't afford to pay for medical services. He gave up luxury to live in poverty so he could serve the needy. That was a virtuous act.

Mother Teresa was a superintendent of a nice Catholic school in middle-class India. She had it made for a comfortable life. Then one day while visiting Calcutta, she saw a person dying on the street without anyone to as much as hold his hand. She said, "No one should have to die alone." So, after getting permission from her superiors, she left the comfort of her school and spent the rest of her life serving the poorest of the poor. When she died, all she owned was five changes of clothing. That was it. Even the hundreds of thousands of dollars she won with the Nobel Peace Prize was given to serve the poor.

There is great virtue when we choose poverty to answer a higher calling. Fulfilling our purpose will require sacrifice of one form or another. It may push us to live in poverty. However, the poverty isn't the virtue. The sacrifice is.

Billy Bob was smarter than most, but he never finished high school because he hated to study. He went to work in construction because it was the only job he could get. Even at that, times had to be really good and builders had to be desperate for Billy Bob to get a job. Billy Bob didn't work too hard. In fact, if the supervisors weren't after him every second, Billy Bob didn't work at all.

Today, nobody wants to be on the job site with Billy Bob because he has a very short fuse and is constantly getting in fights. As soon as he gets off the job, he takes what little money he has, buys beer and cigarettes, and goes home to his little trailer that is falling apart because he doesn't take care of it. There, he spends his evenings on the couch drinking and smoking.

Billy Bob takes great pride in the fact that he isn't materialistic like his cousin William Robert. William Robert kept going to school and going to school and going to school. Eventually, William Robert finished medical school and surgical residency. Now he works long hours saving people's lives. William Robert lives in an exclusive gated community, sends his children to the finest schools, and takes fabulous vacations all over the world.

Who is the virtuous one here? Again, the answer revolves around the sacrifice. Billy Bob doesn't know what it means to sacrifice; as a result, he lives his life in poverty. Billy Bob is no Albert Schweitzer or Mother Teresa. They were poor because they chose to sacrifice. Billy Bob is poor because he chooses NOT to sacrifice.

William Robert has wealth. He can fulfill his purpose in life because he sacrificed. He sacrificed college parties so he could make the grades needed to get into medical school. He sacrificed years of his life and income to make it through medical school.

Yes, William Robert is rich. But that money didn't come from hurting others. It came from year after year of personal sacrifice so that he might best serve others. William Robert's virtue isn't in his money. His virtue, just like Albert Schweitzer or Mother Teresa's, is rooted in his sacrifice.

The point is there is no virtue in poverty. Likewise, there is no virtue in riches. There is only virtue in sacrifice. We sacrifice to achieve wealth so that we can achieve our purpose. Those sacrifices may bring us riches. Or they may leave us with little money in the bank. But sacrifices will never leave us empty-handed because there are always great rewards for success. Let's conclude this book by exploring what these rewards are in the next chapter.

CONCLUSION

*The reason so many people never get anywhere in life is
because, when opportunity knocks, they're out in the
backyard looking for four-leaf clovers.*
—Walter P. Chrysler

THE CHOICE: EASE OR
OPPORTUNITY

There has never been a time in human history when the easy life
was so readily available to us all. Most of us can find a job that's not too
painful. We can put in our time and make enough money to buy a great
entertainment center, stock the fridge, and pay for cable. We can go
to work, come home to the easy chair, and surf the channels. We have
daylong soap operas, nonstop music videos, and year-round sports to
follow. Computers can entertain us with browsers that take us around
the world and games that take us to virtual worlds limited only by our
imaginations. To keep us entertained, we have fantasy baseball. Fantasy
football. And reality TV. We're comfortable. We're well fed. Ah, to come
home to a life with dozens of video games and five hundred TV channels
to choose from. That's the easy life. And that's certainly one option for
living our lives.

On the other hand, there has never been a time in all of human
history when there were as many opportunities for the person willing
to get up out of that easy chair and do something. Going all the way
back to when Adam and Eve were running around in fig leaves, we have
never had the abundance of opportunity that we do today. We can go
where we want to go, do what we want to do, be what we want to be, and
have what we want to have.

We have a choice. Do we choose the easy life, or do we choose the
life of opportunity? If you want a life on easy street, be thankful you are
alive today. Easy street is wider than it has ever been. Settle into the
recliner, grab the remote, and click your way to the life easy. If, on the
other hand, you want a life of opportunity and not ease, still be thankful
you are alive today. Opportunities are easier to find today than they
have ever been.

Easy street it easy to find. Opportunities are also easy to find. However, what we won't find are opportunities on easy street. Great opportunities are there, but they are only there to the person who is willing to face the challenges. The question isn't whether we can find ease or opportunity. The question is "Which one will we choose?"

Is It Worth It?

If we opt for opportunity rather than settle for ease, will it be worth it? Does it really make sense to spend our lives trying to achieve more when what we have isn't that bad?

KEY IDEA

Opportunities are easy to find, but they won't be found on easy street.

In 1972, what Bruce Jenner had wasn't so bad. He surprised those who follow track and field by capturing the third spot on the U.S. Olympic decathlon team. No one even knew who he was, and yet he got to go to the Olympics. He didn't win a medal. He didn't even come close. He didn't expect to. He was just glad he had the chance to compete and be part of the festivities. He had a nice story to tell everyone about what it was like to be an Olympian.

Something happened at the awards ceremonies. His "glad just to be there" attitude changed. As Jenner stood on the field hearing the national anthem of the U.S.S.R. and seeing Nicolay Avilov being crowned as the world's greatest athlete, a question came to his mind. What's the difference between the person standing as champion and the one who is content to be watching from the infield along with the pigeons? Jenner concluded that the difference was total and complete devotion to a purpose.

He decided then and there that he was going to make such a commitment. For the next four years, he would devote every moment of his life to getting where Avilov stood that day. Everything he did would be evaluated against the question of whether it would help him win the gold medal in the decathlon at the next Olympic games.

He went back to his room at the Olympic Village that night to rest from two days of grueling competition. However, he couldn't go to sleep. He laid in bed with the picture of Avilov running through his mind. The only thing he could hear was the ticking of the clock. He realized that with every ticking of the clock, a second had passed. He was one second closer to 1976, the next Olympics. One second had been wasted that he would never get back, a second that could have been spent preparing.

He bolted out of bed, put on his shoes, and took off running through the village. His training began that night, and it did not stop until he achieved his dream. In 1976, Jenner stood on the top step of the podium, a gold medal draped around his neck, while the *Star Spangled Banner* was being played. It took four years of undiluted commitment to a singular goal. It took four years of total sacrifice. It took four years of sweat and toil, pain and agony. It took everything he had, but he won the prize.

Jenner chose opportunity over ease. Was it worth it? Over twenty years later, as Jenner reflected on that question, he wrote:

"When you win, life treats you differently. It opens its arms wide. Yes, life will give you [pain and agony] on the way, but when you win, it gives you everything you can imagine and more."

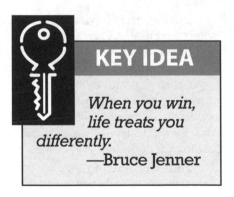

KEY IDEA

When you win, life treats you differently.
—Bruce Jenner

Sure, we can spend our lives in the easy chair, watching TV and living well below our potential. If we do, life will treat us one way. But if we devote ourselves to the pain and struggles of success, life will treat us differently when we win. Life rewards those who win and passes over everyone else.

How does life reward the winners? Let's spend these last few pages together exploring how life treats the winners differently. There are five major rewards of success. Notice the order. We will look at these five major rewards from the least important to the most important.

THE STUFF WE GET

When I was in graduate school, I drove a small economy car that I could barely stuff my six-foot-five-inch body into. I lived in the cheapest efficiency apartment I could find. You've heard of breakfast in bed. My apartment was so small, I could cook breakfast *from* my bed. Then I had to eat it on my bed because there wasn't enough room for

KEY IDEA

The material things we get are the most motivating and the least rewarding part of success.

a table or a chair. I was working hard, but I wasn't experiencing any of the material rewards of success. I continued working, and eventually the rewards came.

Now I enjoy riding in my Lincoln Town Car. I fit better. I like the plush leather seats. They feel better. I have built the office of my dreams at home, which I enjoy a lot. This office is several times larger than the apartment I lived in back in graduate school. I've stuffed it with every electronic toy I can find. I enjoy all the stuff I've gotten from all my years of hard work.

Here's what I have noticed about the material rewards we get from being successful. They are the most motivating and the least rewarding part of success. I have to admit that I didn't decide to pursue a Ph.D. in business because I knew it would give me a deep feeling of fulfillment. I was after the money. I saw these business professors who had great university jobs that paid well. Many of them also had lucrative consulting practices on the side. They lived in nice neighborhoods and drove nice cars. I wanted what they had, so I did what they did. It was the money and the lifestyle that I was after.

There is nothing wrong with letting a desire for the good life motivate us to achieve something. Knowing what we will get if we succeed can push us to try a little harder and work a little longer. It may keep us from giving up and quitting.

Does it sound materialistic or greedy to be motivated by our desires to buy things? I don't think so. When my younger daughter, Alaina, was just seven years old, she decided she wanted a new bicycle, and she was going to earn the money to buy it. She was constantly looking for things she could do to make money. In a few months, she earned her money and she bought the bicycle.

I didn't see my daughter as greedy or materialistic. Quite the opposite. I was proud that I had a daughter who, at seven years of age, had the maturity to set a goal and do what she needed to do to reach it. The same applies to adults who work hard so they can buy nice things. They aren't being greedy or materialistic. They are showing the maturity that it takes to set goals and do what they must to achieve them.

THE THINGS WE GET TO DO

Jonas Salk said, "The greatest reward for doing is the opportunity to do more." People who achieve more have more options. They get to do more things.

Zig Ziglar is in high demand as a speaker. In fact, I heard him tell a group that he hasn't solicited one single speaking engagement in the last thirty years. He commands tens of thousands of dollars per speech. He turns down the vast majority of the speeches that are offered to him. He gets to pick only the ones that really interest him and that won't interfere with the other things he wants to do.

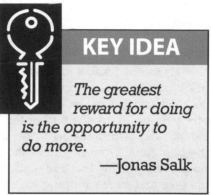

KEY IDEA

The greatest reward for doing is the opportunity to do more.
—Jonas Salk

He didn't start there. He started by taking every speaking engagement that came his way. He would get up at 5:00 a.m. to speak to the people who deliver the bread. He would drive two hours one way at his own expense to talk to a handful of people. Why didn't he accept speaking engagements back then that would put him in front of tens of thousands of people at a time? Because those venues weren't available to him when he was first starting out. Before he was a success, he had to take anything that came his way.

Before we get to do real interesting stuff, we usually have to succeed doing less interesting stuff. That is one of the big rewards for success. Greater opportunities come our way. If we want to cherry-pick the best opportunities, we must first grow the cherry tree. We do that by succeeding.

Who has the more interesting job, the janitor or the CEO? Who has a more interesting day, Bill Gates or the person writing code for Windows? The more success we have, the more interesting our days will be.

I see people waiting for the perfect opportunity to come along before they do anything significant with their lives. They will never do anything. We don't start with perfect opportunities. We are rewarded with perfect opportunities when we do a great job with the less-than-perfect opportunities that come our way.

THE RELATIONSHIPS WE BUILD

There is nothing that bonds two people together more than working together to conquer something. I had a student named Chris who was a professional in tournament fishing. He also worked at a camp for troubled youth. He would take parents and children out on the lake and teach them how to fish. He had incredible results in bringing struggling families back together.

He told me about his first experience doing this. A very successful businessman showed up with his son, who had been in a lot of trouble with the law. When the day started, they weren't even talking to each other. However, by the end of the day, after sharing the experience of fishing and learning how to do it right from a pro, they were having the best time. They caught a bunch of fish, but more importantly, they built a relationship that had never before existed. They immediately left the lake and went shopping for a fishing boat.

The problem with the family was that they didn't have any common experiences to bring them together. The kid wasn't interested in looking over financial statements with his father. The father wasn't interested in playing video games with his son. However, they could come together to conquer the lake.

KEY IDEA

Who attracts the most interesting people into their lives? It's the people who do the most interesting things.

What we do brings us closer to the people who are doing it with us. To build strong friendships, we don't go out looking for friends. We go looking for something significant to do with our lives, and, as a byproduct, the friendships will materialize as we discover fellow travelers along the way.

Who attracts the most interesting people into their lives? It's the people who do the most interesting things. Who does the most interesting things? It's the people who achieve the most. The more we accomplish, the more we find ourselves building bonds with very interesting people.

If I were to get a call from the president of the United States and he said he wanted to spend some time with me, I would be elated. Even if we were at opposite ends of the political spectrum, I would count this as one of the best days of my life. Imagine spending time with someone who had seen what the president sees, experienced what the president experiences, and knows the people the president knows. A few hours with the President would be an experience I would cherish for the rest of my life.

But what if I were secretary of state, and I got a call that the president wanted to spend some time with me? Would that be one of the best days of my life? No. It would be routine. In fact, much of my life would be spent talking to heads of state. Every day, I would spend time with people who had been to incredible places, met interesting people, and impacted a lot of lives. Meeting extremely interesting people would just be part of the job. Someone who achieves the success of a secretary of state spends day after day with real interesting people.

The more we set out to do, the more we build bonds with people who are also doing things with their lives. The more we succeed at what we do, the more we are around people who have also succeeded at what they do. A key to attracting a lot of high-quality people into our lives is to become a high-quality person doing high-quality things.

THE GROWTH WE EXPERIENCE

Here is an interesting thing about life. The more we grow, the better life gets. However, often the only way to grow is to push ourselves to the limits of what we can do. The problem is that we can't enlist our minds to push ourselves to the limits unless we have a strong reason to do so.

In class, I explain to my students the difference between ability and potential. Ability is what we can accomplish with who we are. Potential is what we can accomplish with whom we can become. One day in class, I used push-ups as an example of this. I told my students that I could do about fifty push-ups. No sooner had the words left my mouth than a student challenged me on it. He said, "Okay, do fifty right now." I was in a situation. If I didn't do the push-ups they might not believe anything else I said. So right there, I got down and did fifty push-ups. That is when I discovered that my ability was exactly fifty push-ups. By the time I finished, I am convinced I couldn't have done one more push-up.

But is fifty all the push-ups I could ever do? No. What would happen if I pushed myself to the limit like that on a regular basis? Eventually, I would be able to do fifty-five push-ups. Then sixty. Then sixty-five. My potential is much greater than my current ability.

KEY IDEA

Few of us feel the need to change. Hopefully, we will find something we want that will make us grow to get it.

So, why don't I push myself like that every time I workout? There would be incredible benefits for doing so. Imagine how good of shape I would get into. However, at the gym, I don't have a reason to push past my current ability. Every day when I go to the gym, I don't have forty students watching me wondering if they can trust what I say. So, I may push myself at the gym when I am just working out to stay in shape but not anything like I did that day when I had a bigger reason.

See, here is a benefit of success. To become a success, we have to push ourselves harder. As we do, we become better. We grow. And when we grow, our life becomes better and better.

Throughout this book, a major theme has been that we must grow to achieve our potential. We have discussed it one way or another in every chapter. We said that growth isn't the key to success, but it's the door. We are successful because we grow, and we grow because we are successful. The growth is more important than the success.

It is possible to get the spoils of success without having the growth of success. If we do, it could be one of the worst things to ever happen to us. For example, we might stop by the convenience store on the way home, pick up a pack of cigarettes, a six-pack of beer, and a lottery ticket. Our numbers could pop up and we might become an instant multimillionaire. For a couple of dollars, we could achieve what it takes others years of education, growth, and hard work to accomplish. We have the spoils of success, but we're never refined to be able to deal with them.

It is a rare person who can handle the money without the growth that it takes to earn the money. Chances are better than not that the money would ruin our lives. When I say this in class, I will always get comments like, "Give me the money, I'll take the chance." All that money doesn't solve our problems. It gives us a different set of problems. If we haven't grown to handle this new set of problems, they can bury us. It happens all the time. People win the lottery and it was the event that totally destroyed their lives.

Remember how we said that the things we get from being successful are the most motivating and least rewarding? The opposite is true of growth. Few of us are motivated to grow. We are happy with who we are, and we don't want to change. Hopefully, we want something badly enough that we are willing to change to get it. When we finally do get it, we will be rewarded more for who we become than what we get.

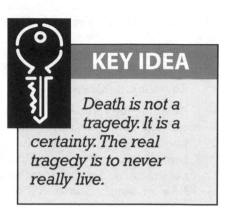

KEY IDEA

Death is not a tragedy. It is a certainty. The real tragedy is to never really live.

THE FULFILLMENT WE FIND

The greatest reward of all for living a successful life is the fulfillment it brings. Hopefully, there will come a point when we look back on our lives and feel very good about what we did with what we had. At that point, we will receive the great reward of knowing that we fulfilled our purpose for being here.

People who have lived the best lives are seldom afraid to die. It is the person who has never accomplished much that fears death. It is as if, somewhere deep inside us, we know we were put on this planet to do something. If we do it, then we are at peace as we face death. If not, then death brings pain and agony. It is the pain and agony of knowing that our purpose was left undone. In Leonardo da Vinci's words, "As a well spent day brings happy sleep, so life well used brings happy death."

We tend to see death as a tragedy. It is not. Death is a certainty. Indeed, there are tragic circumstances surrounding many deaths. Some die way too young. Some deaths seem totally senseless. Some deaths negatively impact the lives of many people. The circumstances of death can be quite tragic, but death itself is not tragic. It is as much a part of life as is birth.

The real tragedy is not to die but to never live. It is tragic when we take the one life given us and thoughtlessly squander it on meaningless activities with no purpose. To have lived and never really lived is the biggest tragedy of all.

In the late 1950s, Dr. Martin Luther King, Jr. was stabbed. The blade came within a fraction of an inch from his aorta. If he would have sneezed, he would have died. Ten years later, King reflected on that experience in a speech. He said that he was glad he didn't die because of the incredible things he was able to experience in the decade since he was stabbed. Indeed, Martin Luther King was sent here to do some incredible things, and he did them in the 1960s.

King closed that speech in a very moving way. He said:

"Well, I don't know what will happen now. We've got some difficult days ahead. But it doesn't matter with me now. Because I've been to the mountaintop and I don't mind. Like anybody, I would like to live a long life. Longevity has its place. But I'm not concerned about that now. I just want to do God's will. And He's allowed me to go up to the mountain. And I've looked over. And I've seen the Promised Land. I may not get there with you. But I want you to know tonight, that we, as a people, will get to the Promised Land. And I'm happy tonight. I'm not worried about anything. I'm not fearing any man. Mine eyes have seen the glory of the coming of the Lord."

Those were the last words King gave from a stage. The next day, an assassin's bullet took his life.

King's death devastated a lot of people. The circumstances of King's death were very tragic—a sick mind thinking he could shut up a divine message by destroying the human messenger. Millions of very good people were badly hurt by this cowardly act.

However, to Martin Luther King himself, death had no sting. He fulfilled his purpose in life. He didn't seek death, but even though he had not yet seen his fortieth birthday, he wasn't afraid to die. He experienced the biggest reward of success. He felt the fulfillment that only comes from knowing that he achieved what he was sent here to do. He saw the Promised Land. He saw his purpose being fulfilled. Having seen it, he faced death with courage. Many years after his death, his purpose moves on. What could be a greater reward for living than that? You don't find that reward on easy street.

BECOMING MY BEST

There you have it—the seven keys to all success. Being a success doesn't mean you can be a success in everything. There are things I can't do, no matter how disciplined I am or how hard I try. That goes for you, too. However, that doesn't matter. I want to find out what I can do ... do it ... and do it to the best of my ability. I don't need to become someone else to be successful. I just need to be constantly becoming a better version of myself. That should be our goal in life. We should strive to achieve what we were meant to achieve by growing into the person we can become.

Let me leave you with a poem I wrote that expresses my deepest aspiration in life. I pray that it is your aspiration, as well.

THE BEST ME I CAN BE

I saw a bird up in the trees
He glided through the air with such great ease.
I wished I could fly like him,
But then I thought that I should think again.
Where I have arms, he has wings;
My hands let me do so many things.
Would I be happy to give mine away?
No, I think the ground is where I'll stay.
I saw a horse that could really run;
To move like that would be so much fun.
I wished I was strong and fast like him,
But then I thought I should think again.
I love to read, learn, and grow;
My books take me places he cannot go.
Would I give all this away?
No, on my two legs is where I'll stay.
All around there are people I see;
Just like them I want to be.
I try so hard to be like them.
I think it's time to think again.
The way I'm created is part of the plan;
I can fulfill my purpose with who I am.
I think that I will just try to see,
That I'm the best me I can be.